PATHS, PATIOS
& DECKING

PATHS, PATIOS & DECKING

PAUL WAGLAND

GUILD OF MASTER
CRAFTSMAN PUBLICATIONS

Dedicated to the memory of Lewis Beckwith.

First published 2011 by
Guild of Master Craftsman Publications Ltd
Castle Place, 166 High Street, Lewes,
East Sussex, BN7 1XU

This title has been created using material previously
published in *Do It – Paths and Patios* (first published 2009)

ISBN 978-1-86108-887-1

Publisher Jonathan Bailey
Production Manager Jim Bulley
Managing Editor Gerrie Purcell
Senior Project Editor Dominique Page
Editors Kevin McRae and Ian Whitelaw
Managing Art Editor Gilda Pacitti
Designer Chloë Alexander

Set in 321impact, Helvetica Neue and Nofret
Colour origination by GMC Reprographics
Printed and bound by Hing Yip Printing Company Ltd in China

Contents

Planning & Design

Building Work

Additions & Improvements | Cleaning & Maintenance

For most of us, relaxation is the number one reason for having a garden. That may mean space to play with the children, somewhere to throw a party or just a comfy sun lounger to enjoy a good book. What we don't need is a garden that takes hours of our time every week and yet, despite our best efforts, never looks 'under control'. You don't have to be a fanatical gardener to really enjoy the great outdoors. Many of the plants and other products available in garden centres are targeted at people who don't have much time to spare – people who want minimum-effort solutions to the problem of keeping a garden tidy throughout the year.

A perfect way to cut your list of weekend chores is to use paving and decking to create versatile and robust areas of 'hard landscaping', which are easy to look after and instantly expand the potential of your garden. Well-designed paths linking the most regularly used parts of the garden cut down on muddy footprints inside the house and make jobs such as picking a few home-grown herbs more pleasant. Even the smallest patio or sun terrace gives you somewhere to entertain friends, and a timber deck is a great way to blur the distinction between inside and outside. Any type, size or style of garden can be improved with a little creative effort, and,

if you choose your design and materials carefully, this type of project should blend seamlessly with the other elements.

It's worth remembering that money spent on such projects is usually a wise investment. Property experts know a well-landscaped garden can increase the value of a house. This is above and beyond the benefit of the 'wow factor' you'll create if the garden is beautifully designed. If your budget is tight, there are still many ways of keeping costs low while maximizing visual appeal. Some projects can be taken on in stages (giving the bank account a chance to recover), while others may require only inexpensive materials and little or no professional help.

The four main sections of this book cover designing, constructing, furnishing and maintaining paths and patios. But there is no need to read the whole book before starting work. Each stage is considered separately, so if you already have a firm idea of what you want to achieve, skip section one – which covers design – and go straight to building work in section two. If you have a patio but want to make more of it, concentrate on sections three and four. Whatever your goals and circumstances, the aim of this book is to provide you with the inspiration and knowledge required for a great result.

Even before you draw up your plans, you should make sure you
have a clear idea of what you want from your patio or path – how
you intend to use it, how you would like it to work with the rest of
your garden and how much time and money you are prepared
to put into it. Once you have sorted out these issues, you can
concentrate on the design of the paved area, deciding on the
site, type of surface and features you would like.

Planning & Design

Before you begin

I'S NOT a coincidence that garden makeovers on television always start with sorting out the hard landscaping. This is perhaps the most important aspect of garden design – and certainly the one that's hardest to change once it's done. Hard landscaping acts as a background for every element of the garden and, if done well, facilitates easy access to other areas.

Tough criteria

PRESSURES ON time and space mean gardens are often required to fulfil many different roles. Today's typical plot might need to contain boisterous children or pets safely, feed the local wildlife, provide fruit and vegetables and extend living and entertaining space, while looking beautiful throughout most of the year. This might seem a tall order, but, with careful planning, it's quite possible to design a garden that meets all these demands – and a structural 'backbone' of paving should be top of the wish list for anyone who wants a useful, versatile garden.

A key feature

Central to most garden designs is the patio, which not only creates the perfect environment for an al fresco meal or a few drinks (with or

▼ **The perfect way to spend a summer morning – with a paper and breakfast on a well-designed patio.**

without friends and family) but is also a very low-maintenance area that can be dressed with furniture and container plants as the occasion or season requires. It also blurs the boundaries between the indoor and outdoor areas of your home, encouraging you to make more use of outside space whatever the weather. It can even be useful in helping to keep muddy footprints out of the house.

▲ Hard landscaping allows you to make more of your outside space in all weathers.

▶ Your choice can give a distinct flavour to your garden, from the peaceful English countryside to the sunny Mediterranean.

▼ Even the smallest terrace can transform the way you use your garden, inviting you out into the fresh air.

Are you up to the job?

PEOPLE OFTEN think of hard landscaping as difficult, unpleasant work, but, in most cases, this is far from the reality. Even the greenest do–it–yourself novice can lay a simple path in a few hours, and more complex tasks – such as building steps or walls – are well within the capabilities of anyone with a reasonable level of physical fitness. As with most such projects, the key lies in having the self–confidence to get

▲ **Even simple paving and minimal elegant furniture can have a transformative effect on your garden.**

started; after that you will find that the work is much simpler than you thought. It's certainly worth the effort: estate agents and property experts estimate that a well landscaped garden can add 10 per cent or more to the value of a property, and an entertaining area such as a deck or patio can appreciably improve the appearance of the outside of your house.

Cost and quality

There's no denying you can pay a fortune for high–quality paving materials, but there is also a wide range of more sensibly priced alternatives on offer. Reconstituted stone was once sneered at, but the stuff on sale today in every builders' yard or DIY retailer is almost indistinguishable from natural stone and is a fraction of the price – not to mention being easier to lay and less prone to staining. It is worth keeping in mind that paving will probably last for many years – and will reduce the time needed for maintaining your garden during that period – so don't let the initial cost of materials put you off. It's usually wise to opt for the best possible materials that you can afford. (See page 26 for help with planning your budget.)

> ## Top tip
>
> You can cut down your material costs by designing paths and patios according to the dimensions of the materials from which they are made. Timber, for example, often comes in multiples of 600mm, so why not build your deck 3m wide, and cut down on wastage? The same consideration applies to paving.

A question of style

MOST KEEN gardeners have a personal style that influences their decisions. You may think of yourself as a 'natural' gardener, interested in looking after local wildlife, probably using organic techniques, and not being too upset by the occasional pile of fallen leaves. Alternatively, you may prefer a more contemporary approach, with sharply defined surfaces and chic swathes of colour-coordinated planting. You might have chosen to follow a favourite theme, such as a traditional cottage garden or a soft-toned Mediterranean courtyard.

There for the asking

Whichever school of thought you follow, there will be a style of paving to suit. Specialist hard-landscaping companies produce sumptuous catalogues packed cover to cover with different colours, designs and qualities of paving, and recent years have seen a boom in the market for patio kits – and other ready-made materials – that can be bought 'off-the-shelf' from any DIY store. Even cement is now easier to purchase; you can get it in a bag already mixed with ballast so you simply need to add a little water.

▼ **Clever use of materials can help to blend new paving with the rest of the garden.**

Considering possibilities

ONE OF the chief advantages of using hard-landscaping materials (from natural stone to loose gravel or even timber) is that they can be made to fit any shape, large or small, in any part of the garden. Most people would want a patio close to their lounge or kitchen to make entertaining easier, but there's no reason not to create other spaces elsewhere. Imagine a sunny, secluded spot, out of sight of the rest of the house, paved with natural stone and sheltered by scented climbers and flower-laden

▶ **Plan your paving at the earliest stage of garden design and fit other elements in around it.**

▼ **The conditions around an enclosed patio allow you to grow plants that appreciate warmth and sunlight.**

▲ If privacy is important and you wish to create a
visual barrier, be sensitive to your neighbours' needs.

▶ Do you wish to entertain large groups of people,
or do you simply want to create an intimate space
for relaxation?

obelisks – the perfect place to read a good book
on a summer's afternoon. Or, for the water
gardener, how about an elegant timber deck,
one side lined with whispering silver birch
and the other hovering gracefully over the
still water of your pond? The possibilities are
limited only by the scope of your imagination.

Drawing up your design

REDESIGNING YOUR garden can be an exciting project, and one that can allow you many opportunities to express your creativity. To achieve the best results, however, it is often worth reining in your enthusiasm a little and taking your time. Before you set your heart on a particular idea, make sure that you have thoroughly researched all your options and considered any difficulties that may arise.

▼ **Geometry is an important tool in design, but don't use it too rigidly or the garden will look unnatural.**

Seeking the muse

IF YOU find the creative process doesn't come naturally, and you are struggling for ideas, visit gardens nearby that are open to the public. Failing this, there are a number of magazines that specialize in the design side of gardening and are an excellent source of inspiration. Don't be at all afraid to copy elements of someone else's design, or even to lift whole schemes and adapt them to your own circumstances.

▲ **Always consider what the focal point of the garden will be. A circular patio can really catch the eye.**

▼ **Tie the look of the garden into existing features, and avoid using too many different colours or textures.**

Assessing your garden

YOUR FIRST job in creating a design is to take stock of what's in your garden already, deciding what you want to keep, what needs to be removed and what you need to add to improve the overall design. Take a week or so to walk all over the plot at different times of day, making notes about everything that strikes you as important. Where are the major trees, and how do they cast shade? Which parts of the garden need to be accessed easily, and from where? Do you need to be able to

▼ **When you are planning the overall layout, consider how each part of the garden will be accessed or viewed from other areas.**

watch over children while they play on the lawn or patio? If so, can you see this part of the garden from the lounge or kitchen window?

Getting there

Paths are usually installed as a means of access to another part of the garden rather than as an end in their own right, but the route itself is still an important consideration. Do you want simply to get where you're going as quickly as possible, or would you prefer to meander through flowerbeds and under trees, smelling and touching the plants as you go? A patio, on the other hand, is in itself a destination and meant to be enjoyed for longer periods of time. The physical comfort of those using it is therefore of much more importance and needs to be carefully considered.

Things to consider while planning

Aspect

Sunshine is important to the enjoyment of your garden, so take note of which areas are in sun or shade at different times of the day. A patio that faces due south will receive sunshine for most of the day, while east- or west-facing plots will be sunny in the morning or evening respectively. Avoid building a patio against a north-facing wall – it's unlikely to see much use. Don't forget that shadows will be much longer in winter than in summer, as the sun is lower in the sky.

Exposure

Just as the sun warms us, so the wind can cool us down. The prevailing wind in the United Kingdom comes from the southwest, but the coldest and strongest winds come from the north and east. Bear this in mind when choosing the location of a patio, and look for a place that is well sheltered – or can at least be made so through the use of protective planting.

Privacy

It is important to consider which areas can be seen by your neighbours or the public, and whether there is anything you can do about this with trelliswork or hedging. Nobody likes to be overlooked while they relax with a glass of wine and a book, and there's a lot of truth in the old saying 'good fences make good neighbours'.

Topography

This means simply 'the way the land slopes'. A change in the level of the site makes landscaping technically more difficult, but also presents many opportunities in terms of design. Steps, terraces and retaining walls open up a whole new range of options for features in your garden.

Sight lines

On a small plot, you will probably be able to see every part of your garden from every other, but, if you are lucky enough to have a larger area to play with, the view from each part of the garden is something you should consider. If you don't have the luxury of a glorious view across the countryside, you can create your own view by planting the rest of the garden so it looks beautiful from your seat on the patio.

▼ **Hard landscaping can blur the distinction between inside and outside space, but should be carefully planned to maximize its potential.**

Choosing your surface

▲ With its irregularities and soft tones, natural stone undeniably has a feel and quality all of its own.

▲ Used judiciously, concrete paving slabs are an excellent option for those on a budget.

Natural stone

Perhaps the most luxurious option, real stone slabs can look truly wonderful and are not as expensive as they used to be, thanks to increased competition among suppliers. They are still not a cheap material, however, and you should work out your budget carefully before you place your order. As with all natural materials, stone can be a little variable in terms of the dimensions and finish – so be aware that laying a stone patio may require a bit more thought than would be needed for other surfaces. Watch out also for chisel marks and other cosmetic damage caused during the quarrying process; such details are not necessarily unattractive (and can even be a feature) but some people will prefer to have them on the underside. Some types of stone are difficult to keep clean and may be more prone to staining, but you can buy various proprietary sealants that can simply be painted over the stone. These may be sold as specific to a certain stone (such as slate or limestone) and can change the appearance of the finished surface slightly – try them out on a small, discreet area first.

Concrete and reconstituted stone

Hugely popular, concrete paving is cheap and easy to lay (thanks to its uniform shape), and is now much more appealing than the ugly grey slabs that used to be so prevalent. It is available in an almost limitless range of colours, and is often sold in the form of 'patio kits' that allow you to build a given size of paved square, rectangle or circle straight from a pre-prepared pallet. If you want a long-lasting, simple-to-lay patio that

won't break the bank then this could be the way forward. On the downside, concrete slabs are not as warm-looking as bricks or setts, and with real stone coming down in price it may be tempting to splash out. It is also possible to buy reconstituted stone slabs, which are made from the dust and chippings produced in quarries. These are very similar in every respect to the concrete variety but give you a little more choice when it comes to appearance. If colour is an important part of your design, ask the supplier if you can take a single slab home as a sample, and compare this to the other materials in your garden.

Bricks and setts

For a warm, relaxed and cosy feel, it is hard to beat salvaged bricks. You can pick them up from any reclaim yard, but sadly they are now becoming rather expensive. Modern bricks may be cheaper and can look great if you avoid the bottom of the range. Another option is to use stone or concrete setts (sometimes called block paving), which are similar to bricks but tend to be smaller and squarer in shape. The technique

▼ By using bricks that match those of your house, you can instantly achieve an integrated look for your patio.

Top tip

By matching the materials you use in the new construction to those that are already on the site (such as those of a house or garden walls) you will instantly make your project blend in.

required to lay either is different from that used for larger slabs (which require more stability) but is not difficult. Indeed, bricks and setts are easier to work with if lifting heavy weights is a problem for you, and there is more scope for personal creativity – you can easily create patterns with lines of different-coloured materials. One drawback is that there are many more joints between the paving elements, and these are often pointed with loose sand. As a result weeds can take hold more easily than on a slabbed patio with mortar joints.

Timber decking

A quick and attractive finish that is within the reach of all but the least experienced DIYer, decking has become so popular that there are numerous companies offering off-the-peg decking kits, components and accessories. While this makes installation a doddle, it is not a great deal more work to build a bespoke design to fit a specific situation. Decking is cheaper than stone or concrete – but perhaps not by as much as you might expect. It's fairly easy to adapt a deck once

▼ **Timber decking can provide a solution if you face the challenge of wildly uneven ground.**

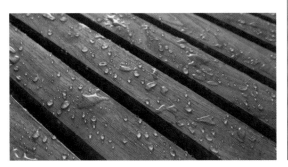

it is built – for example, if you want to create a new 'island planting' area or drill holes to run pipework or electrics.

It is also an excellent way to deal with a sloping site, as the supporting posts can hold the finished surface above the ground, which obviates the need for you to excavate a terrace. The downsides of this option are that it doesn't last as long as stone, needs regular maintenance (cleaning yearly, painting or staining around every two years) and can become unsightly and even dangerously slippery when it gets wet.

Loose aggregates

Generally the cheapest option, 'loose' materials such as gravel, woodchip or shredded bark are also some of the simplest materials from which to create a patio area. The easiest construction involves a boundary of timber boards with weed-suppressing membrane laid inside.

On top of this is spread a layer of the chosen surface material, usually to a depth of at least 50mm. Besides price and ease of installation, the other advantages include the particulate nature of the material (which allows you to fill awkward corners and curves with little extra effort); the security aspect of having crunchy, noisy gravel around the perimeter of your house; or the safety factor of soft, impact-absorbing woodchip or bark.

The downsides are that the material can be blown or kicked around and may look scruffy after time; that weeds may quickly take hold (particularly in bark); and that the surface can become uneven, needing regular raking to flatten it out.

▼ **Patios and paths that are made of loose materials are the most easily installed but are likely to require the most maintenance.**

Levels of design

CHANGES IN level provide both a challenge and an opportunity when sorting out your design. Steps and a retaining wall are one option for creating different levels, but you could use the opportunity to create contrasting areas. A stylish patio could, for instance, give way to a more informal part of the garden via an elegant set of steps. Once the overall plan is ready, think about the detailing, such as how to integrate any structures positioned on the hard landscaping – an arbour or a gazebo, for example.

▶ **Using gravel around pillars can help you avoid having unsightly cut slabs, and leaves open the possibility of planting climbers.**

▼ **The clean lines of a stone retaining wall and staircase are continued in a low wall around the flowerbed below.**

▶ **Two sets of semi-circular steps lead the eye from the geometry of the patio up to a well-tended lawn and on into nature.**

Working out a budget

AFTER YOU'VE come up with an initial design for your project, but before you make any firm decisions or order the materials, it's a wise move to work out an approximate budget. This will not only bring into focus the costs required but will also be useful in helping you to decide where your funds are best directed.

The table opposite will help you think through the costs involved but is not a complete guide to every expense you may incur. Your individual situation may throw up other considerations, which you'll need to plan for (sometimes unexpectedly – if you discover a drain where you didn't know one existed, for example), and there may be several aspects of the table that don't apply to you at all. Just take what you need and add to it as you see fit.

▼ **Even a small space can be filled with interest – the key here is to keep the design simple.**

Tools

Purchase .... £_____
Hire .... £_____
Safety equipment .... £_____

Excavation

Skip delivery and removal .... £_____
Mini digger (and driver?) .... £_____

Sub-base construction

Plate compactor .... £_____
Hardcore .... £_____
Sand .... £_____
Gravel .... £_____
Cement .... £_____
Concrete – ready-mixed .... £_____

Surfaces

Paving slabs .... £_____
Brickwork .... £_____
Setts .... £_____
Aggregates .... £_____
Edging .... £_____

Lighting

Lamp fittings .... £_____
Cables .... £_____
Accessories .... £_____

Water features

Pond liner material .... £_____
Pumps and filters .... £_____
Plants and fish .... £_____

Furniture and accessories

Patio table and chairs .... £_____
Bench seating and/or hammock .... £_____
Barbecue .... £_____
Fire pit or patio heater .... £_____
Sculpture and other decoration .... £_____

Professional help

Garden designer or
landscape architect .... £_____
Surveyor .... £_____
Labourers or groundworkers .... £_____
Landscape gardener .... £_____
Bricklayer .... £_____
Electrician .... £_____
Carpenter .... £_____
Decorator .... £_____

Subtotal .... £_____

Contingency fund

Add 10% of total budget .... £_____

Total .... £_____

Making a plan

ONCE YOU'VE assessed your garden, make a scale plan of the whole area. An easy way to do this is to use 1cm graph paper and allow, say, four squares per metre (a scale of 1:25). While you're working outdoors, it can be difficult to keep your plan neat, so write all measurements down on a rough sketch and create a final version once indoors.

Level gardens

1 USING a surveyor's tape measure – and a helpful friend – measure and draw the outer boundaries of your plot.

2 NOW work inwards, marking every permanent feature, including flowerbeds, trees, buildings, ponds, walls and fences. Take the time to be accurate, as your measurements will affect everything you do from now on **A**.

A

Top tip

It's all too easy to start thinking in just two dimensions when working on a plan. Remember your site has a vertical aspect too, so highlight this with changes in level, arbours, obelisks and taller plants.

Sloping gardens

1 IF you have a sloping plot, measure out the areas as described above, and try to keep the tape horizontal when you do, as the diagonal line will be longer.

2 NOW work out the gradient of the slope using a vertical stick or cane and a long spirit level **B**. Measure a set horizontal distance (perhaps 2m) out from the top of the slope, then measure the distance from the end of the horizontal line to the ground. Convert this into a simple gradient; for example, a drop of 25cm over a distance of 2m is a gradient of 1:8. This is a tricky thing to draw on your plan, but make a note of it and keep it in mind while designing.

B

Patio/deck planner

USE THE grid below as a starting point for planning your patio or deck. Make some enlarged photocopies of this page (enlargements of 150 per cent will fit onto A3 paper) and use one copy to draw up the final plan of your patio or deck, making sure it is

to scale (one square = 500mm). Then cut out the example furniture and plants you want to include in your garden from some of the other copies. You can then move these around on your plan to try out different layouts.

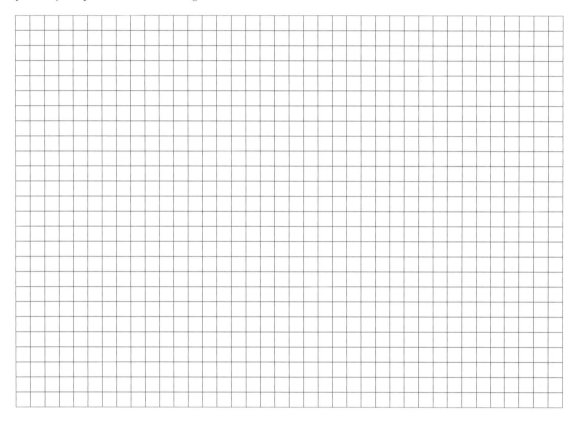

Patio umbrella

Sun lounger

Barbecue

Chair

Large pot plant

Small pot plant

Circular table, four people

Square table, four people

Rectangular table, six or eight people

Bench, two to three people

Hammock

creating a new design

THE PROCESS of sorting out all your ideas can seem somewhat daunting if you are new to designing. The most important thing, however, is to remember that, at this stage, you basically have nothing to lose but a few sheets of paper. There are a number of different ways you can approach the design process.

Option 1

1 USE your completed plan of the existing garden and simply start drawing **A**.

2 ONCE you've made a start, you can gradually refine and improve your ideas until you are happy with the final design **B**.

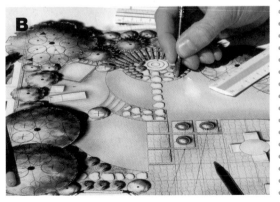

Option 2

1 LAY tracing paper over a copy of your existing garden plan so you can sketch in new elements without redrawing the whole site each time you make a mistake.

2 SWITCH to a new sheet of tracing paper to try a different idea and overlay multiple sheets to combine different concepts.

3 WHEN you've decided which of your ideas work best, simply trace them onto a final master plan.

Option 3

1 MAKE paper cutouts, correctly scaled, of sheds, patio furniture or any other design element of a known size and shape. (See page 29 for a range of graphics of patio furniture that you can photocopy and cut out.)

2 MOVE these around in your design to see how they'll fit without having to mark your plans.

Option 4

1 HAVING completed one of the first three options – if you really feel your creative juices flowing – you might want to build a scale model of your design so you can check the heights of trees and buildings and how they will cast shadows.

2 MOVE a torch around the model to simulate the path of the sun.

Setting out the site

JUST AS it is important to make an accurate plan of the existing site, it is also crucial that you take care over marking out the finished design. Errors at this stage can be expensive and time-consuming to fix once the physical work begins.

1 IF any obstructions need to be removed – such as unwanted plants, old stonework or timber – do this before you begin.

2 USE a fixed point of reference, such as the corner of a building, and measure everything out from there, rechecking each dimension against those around it.

3 USE timber pegs and string to mark out straight lines, and a length of hosepipe, a line of sand or temporary marking paint to

Top tip

If you need to leave the markings for a while, always assume that they have been tampered with, and check them again before you start the actual building work.

define any curves **A**. Make sure that marker pegs are driven firmly into the ground so they can't be accidentally knocked out of place **B**.

4 WALK around the site once it has been marked out. Try to visualize how your patio will look once it is complete, to work out if each area is where it should be and if access will be comfortable.

Tools and equipment

HAVING THE right tools is essential if you want to do a good job. Most tools required for hard landscaping are cheap to buy, but if you intend to use them often it is well worth buying the best tools your budget will allow.

Hiring equipment

WHILE IT is advisable to purchase most of the tools you will need, some – such as plate compactors, cement mixers or mini diggers – are expensive and used only for specialized purposes. Therefore they are probably best hired from a plant-hire company for a weekend or two. Look through the Yellow Pages for any that are in your area and ring a few to get an idea of prices. Such tools are specifically mentioned in the text at points where they might be useful.

Skip hire

Since you will probably need to get rid of a lot of soil and other waste material, you should consider hiring a skip. Again, the Yellow Pages will provide the details of local skip-hire

companies. Do keep in mind the fact that you will need somewhere to have the skip 'dropped', and, if this is on a public road, you will need to pay extra for a council permit to do this (though the paperwork will be handled by the skip-hire company).

You should also work out in advance how large the skip needs to be – remember that soil can double in volume when excavated. Skips come in various sizes – commonly two, four or six cubic metres. The hire company will be able to advise you on the most suitable one for your needs.

▼ **A mini digger makes light work of excavating foundations, but plan where the soil will go before you start.**

CAUTION: SKIP HIRE

- If a skip is to be parked on the public road, then you will need a skip licence from your local authority.

- The skip must be marked by amber flashing lights, either placed against the skip or attached to each corner.

- There must be traffic cones on the approach side of the skip to guide the traffic safely past. It is usually the responsibility of the hire company to provide the lights and cones.

The necessary tools

Safety equipment and clothing

Overalls – or at least strong, rough clothes
Gloves
Boots – steel–toed
Particle mask
Eye goggles
Ear protectors

Surveying tools

Long spirit level
Surveyor's tape measure
5m tape measure
Pegs and string
Graph paper
Pencils
Compass
Builder's square (also known
as folding square)

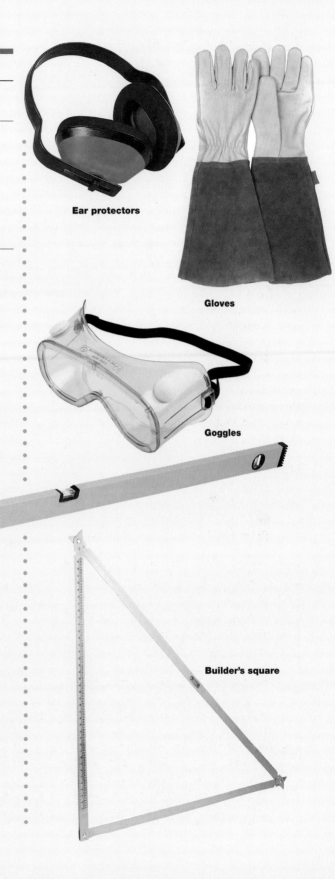

Ear protectors

Gloves

Goggles

Long spirit level

5m tape measure

Builder's square

Excavating and groundwork tools

Digging spade
Digging fork
Shovel
Pickaxe
Wheelbarrow
Garden trowel
Rake
Sledgehammer
Plate compactor
Garden roller
Skip

Tools for stone and brick

Club hammer
Brick hammer
Brick bolster
Cold chisel
Angle grinder
Mason's trowel
Pointing trowel
Rubber mallet
Builder's line
Pins
Bucket
Spacers
Plugging chisel
Cement mixer
Mini digger

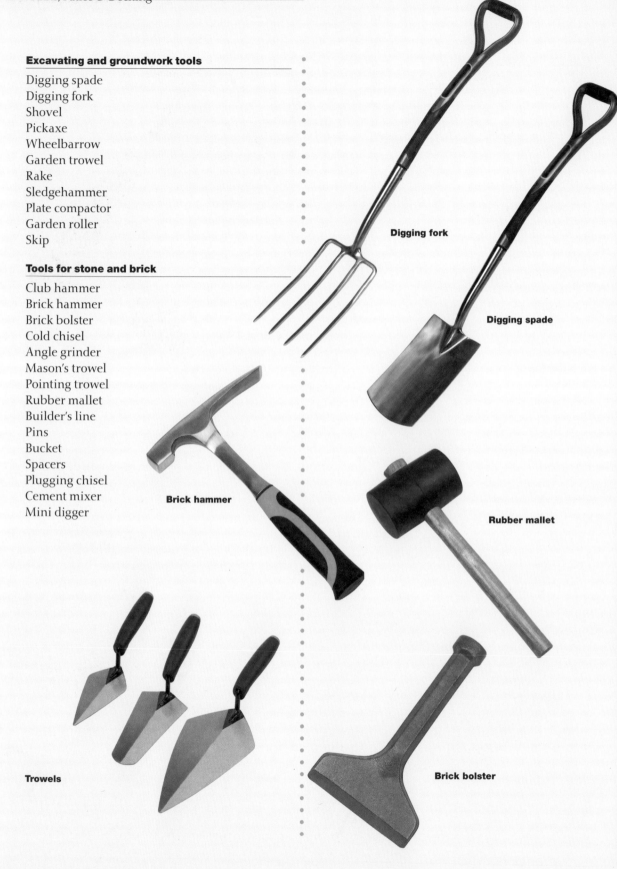

Digging fork

Digging spade

Brick hammer

Rubber mallet

Trowels

Brick bolster

Tools for timber

Handsaw
Cordless jigsaw
Claw hammer
Combination square
Bradawl
Screwdrivers
Timber chisels

Other useful items

Cordless drill/driver with a range of bits
Stanley knife
Pliers
Adjustable spanners
Paintbrush
Broom
Dustpan and stiff brush

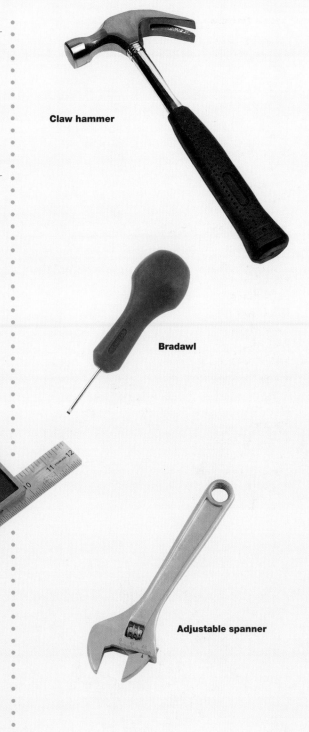

Claw hammer

Bradawl

Combination square

Adjustable spanner

CAUTION: SAFETY AT WORK

- No matter how experienced you are at DIY, it pays to think about the possible dangers involved in any work you do. Moving large quantities of stone and earth can be physically demanding. As you tire, your attention can wander, and this will put your safety, and that of those around you, at risk.

- Simply lifting a spadeful of earth can be enough to damage your back, if you're not used to such work – or you don't warm up properly. Remember to bend your knees rather than your back, and don't be too proud to ask friends for help.

- Many of the tools listed in the checklist on the previous pages can be dangerous if you use them incorrectly. If you're not entirely sure about the best way to go about something, take the time to figure it out first – or ask an expert for advice. Most DIY stores and builders' merchants will have someone on their staff who will be able to tell you how you should proceed.

- Wearing the right clothing is a crucial part of working safely. Safety equipment doesn't have to be uncomfortable or expensive. In fact, it could save a great deal of discomfort in the long term. Strong 'rough' clothes are a good start, but overalls are ideal for many jobs, and steel-toed wellingtons provide invaluable protection when installing heavy paving. You'll only need to drop one paving slab on your foot before you find out why!

Power tool safety

- Power tools are an area of particular concern when considering safety. If an accident is going to happen with power tools, it will happen fast. It's obviously important to take precautions – not only to avoid injury to oneself and others but also to avoid damage to tools and materials. While each machine or tool has its own idiosyncrasies, there are nevertheless general safety procedures that are common to all, and any person who engages in DIY would be wise to become familiar with these to the point where they are second nature.

- Do not wear loose clothing or jewellery, and, if necessary, tie back long hair. Anything that could get caught up in moving parts is an accident waiting to happen.

- Do not operate machinery when tired, drunk or taking medication.

- Use appropriate protective wear. In most operations involving power tools, there is likely to be debris thrown off, so wear some form of eye shield. If the job involves dust, wear a dust mask. Working with machines can be noisy, so wear some form of ear protection – ear defenders or simple earplugs.

- The work area should be dry, clean, well lit and tidy. There should not be anything to cause a trip or a slip. Children and pets must be kept out of the way.

- Inspect all tools regularly for signs of wear and damage. Check carefully for any scorch marks, loose screws, nicks in the cable, exposed wires and so on. Check that a motor's air slots are clean and free of debris. Cutting edges must be sharp, and blade guards should operate properly.

- Avoid starting power tools unintentionally. Unplug them when not in use – particularly if you are adjusting them or changing accessories or attachments. Never carry them with your finger on the trigger or by holding the cable.

- Use sensible techniques. Either the tool or the work must be secure. When force is applied through a hand-held tool to an unsteady work piece, there is a good chance that something will slip.

- Check that the path of the cut is clear of obstructions, including the hidden side. Make sure the cable is out of harm's way. If you are using a hand-held power tool, drape it over your shoulder.

- Take a firm stance, holding the tool away from the body but do not overreach.

- Wait until the motor of a power tool reaches full speed before applying it to the work piece.

- Always adhere to manufacturers' instructions.

- Finally, stay alert, use common sense and never take risks.

Among the simplest ways to improve a garden, a well-designed patio, terrace or deck will add far more to the value of your home than the cost of the materials involved. Paths too, though often overlooked as a design element, are crucial to the success of any garden – whether they are purely practical or designed with leisurely strolling in mind. Remember, however, that the key to any successful paving project is strong foundations; building these may be physically hard, but it is straightforward and will need to be done only once.

Building Work

Preparing a foundation

THE FIRST task in creating any patio or path is building the foundation. A well–constructed foundation will prevent your paved area from shifting – and, potentially, breaking up – at a later date, so choosing the right type for your project is very important. It's not a tricky choice, however. For timber decking on a flat surface, you can probably manage without any foundation at all – and even a raised deck over damp or uneven ground will only require small concrete pads. Also, if your aim is simply to create an area of gravel or other soft aggregate, you can often get away with removing the turf, compacting the soil and laying the surface material directly onto a layer of weed–excluding membrane or landscaping fabric.

However, for longer–lasting paths and patios, areas that will take regular use or anywhere that will be paved with bricks, setts or stone, you should take the time to excavate and install a proper foundation. This should comprise compacted hardcore topped with blinding (a thin layer of compacted sand, to fill any holes) and then a final layer of sand or concrete.

▼ **Groundwork can be messy and disruptive, but it is usually over in a day or two.**

Anatomy of a foundation

There's no denying that building foundations is hard work, but it is worth putting the effort in and doing it well first time around. This will avoid future problems with movement – a situation that would be much more difficult and costly to put right.

The diagram below shows how a typical foundation is constructed. Remember to allow for the thickness of your paving material when building a foundation, so that the surface of the patio finishes flush with the surrounding ground.

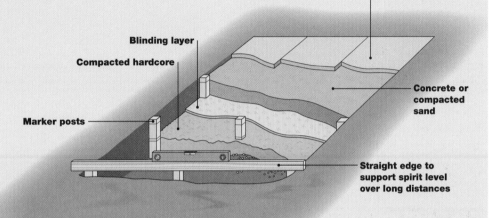

Paving material

Blinding layer

Compacted hardcore

Marker posts

Concrete or compacted sand

Straight edge to support spirit level over long distances

Setts

While bricks do make good paving materials, they are, of course, actually designed for building walls. A more tailored product, which has advantages over bricks as a result, is the sett. Setts are usually (but not always) something close to a cube in shape, with a square upper surface and rather more depth than a brick. This means they are less prone to cracking under pressure, though may take slightly longer to lay, simply because you need more of them per given area. Their depth means that they resist movement well when laid tightly together in a bed of sand, though for an extra-secure result you could lay them in mortar.

Measuring up

THE MOST important aspect of excavating a foundation is getting the depth right. If you dig too deep, you'll either need to pay for more materials to fill the hole or your paving will finish below the ideal level. On the other hand, if your excavations are too shallow, you will end up with paving that either stands clear of the surrounding ground or has a weak sub–base. To work out how deep to dig, first decide where you want the finished 'ground level' to be. This might simply be level with the surrounding lawn or an existing area of hard landscaping. If a building will abut the paving, use it as a frame of reference, and don't build anything higher than 150mm below the damp–proof course, or you'll get damp problems inside. The required distance between the finished surface and the bottom of the excavation depends on the type of paving you intend to use, and is best marked out with timber marking posts.

Anatomy of a marker post

Making marker posts is the easiest way to ensure your levels remain correct when laying paving. Any timber offcuts could be used, but sturdy posts, 450mm long, are the best option. Roughly excavate the footings, then drive your posts into the ground until the tops are flush with the desired finished surface. Remove extra soil as required, then add the sub-base materials layer by layer, each time working to the relevant line on your posts.

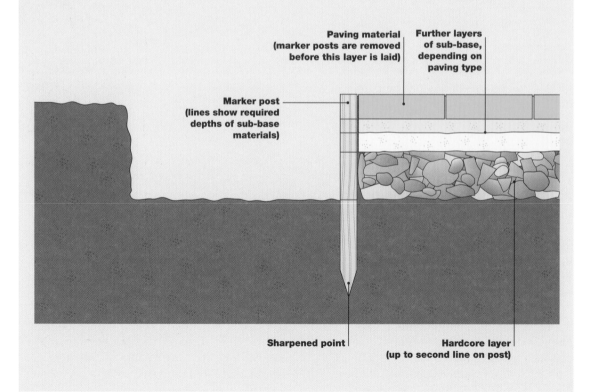

Paving material (marker posts are removed before this layer is laid)

Further layers of sub-base, depending on paving type

Marker post (lines show required depths of sub-base materials)

Sharpened point

Hardcore layer (up to second line on post)

Making marker posts

1 MARK out and cut a series of 450mm lengths from 25 x 25mm pieces of timber.

2 STARTING from the top, mark each of your posts to allow for the thickness of your paving slabs – plus another 25mm if you are setting it in mortar.

3 MAKE a second mark 50mm below this to allow for a layer of sand or concrete (depending on your construction method).

4 FINALLY, make a third mark that is a further 100mm down to make room for the compacted hardcore **A**.

Creating a fall

WHEN MEASURING up the foundations for any paved area it is important to incorporate the necessary fall into your calculations. A fall, as you might expect, is a change in level from one part of the site to another. At the design stage, it can refer to an existing drop (such as across a grass area, over which you wish to pave) but it is used here to describe a deliberate slope in a paved surface, created to allow rainwater to run off into flowerbeds or borders. Patios and paths made from porous materials, such as gravel

or chipped bark, won't need a fall, but stone or brick patios will, otherwise rainwater will pool on your paving, which may also stain the surface.

To create a fall, you will need a shim. This is nothing more than a small piece of wood, cut to a specific size, that will allow you to drive your marker posts to exactly the right depth. The size of the shim you use will depend on the fall you need to create, which in turn depends on the type of surface that you are building. The table overleaf gives appropriate falls for each type of paved surface.

The necessary fall

Surface	Fall	Drop per 1m	Drop per 1.5m
Driveway	1 in 40 (away from walls)	25mm	38mm
Patio	1 in 60 (away from walls)	17mm	25mm
Footpath	1 in 80 (across width)	12.5mm	19mm

Anatomy of a fall

Creating a fall seems like a really tricky job, but a simple piece of timber called a shim makes it very straightforward. A shim is cut to exactly the right size to represent the distance your paving should fall after a given distance (ideally the distance between your marker posts). By placing it on top of the lower marker post and then ensuring the top of the shim is level with the top of the upper marker post, you can be sure the fall is correct.

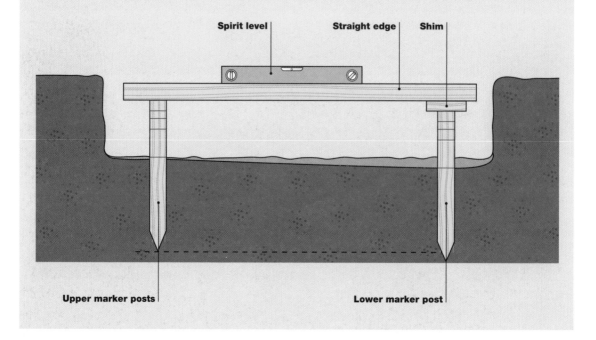

Spirit level | Straight edge | Shim

Upper marker posts | Lower marker post

The digging work

EXCAVATING FOUNDATIONS is not a task for anyone who isn't reasonably fit, but, if you can run for the bus with a few shopping bags, you can probably manage. Remember to take plenty of breaks, and keep yourself shaded and well hydrated in hot weather. If you need to remove more earth than you can find a home for elsewhere in the garden, be sure to book a skip in advance (see page 32). If you leave it until after you've done the digging, you'll have to wait for the skip to arrive and then move the soil a second time.

Hired help

If you don't feel up to the job, or have a very large area to excavate, most tool–hire companies will be able to offer (or at least recommend) the services of a mini digger, sometimes complete with a trained driver. While this can involve a bit of money, it is well worth it when you think of the time and effort it could save you. One thing to consider is access to the site, as a 1.5–tonne piece of plant machinery isn't easy to lift over a neighbour's fence!

Compacting material

For hard landscaping of areas larger than 4m², it really is worth hiring a plate compactor (or 'whacker') to compact the various layers of your sub–base and to bed down setts or bricks laid loose into sand. Plate compactors work by vibrating a heavy metal plate in contact with the ground, squashing your materials into a firm mass and making them much less likely to shift or settle.

If you don't want to stretch the budget to a plate compactor, at least think about hiring a garden roller. Fill this with water once it's on site and wheel it back and forth across the materials you wish to compact.

▼ **A plate compactor is useful for preparing soil, hardcore or sand for whatever needs to be laid on top.**

Temporary paths

THERE WILL be times while you are building your patio when you will need to transport large quantities of materials across your garden – both as you take away soil and as you bring in materials such as hardcore and sand. This will tend to involve lots of traffic back and forth – perhaps with a wheelbarrow or other heavy equipment – which can be disastrous for your carefully manicured lawn. The answer is to use a temporary path that will protect the grass from harm but can then be easily removed once the job is done.

Spreading the load

A traditional approach is to use wide timber planks (scaffold boards are ideal) laid in a line between two points. A modern option, and one that may be easier to store away, is a plastic roll–out path made of linked sections, something like a caterpillar track. The function of both is to spread the load of the traffic across a larger area, so you're not left with a muddy trench when the job is done. Even after you have finished the building work, temporary paths can be useful, perhaps to take prunings away from an unruly tree or hedge or to make repairs to part of the structure of the garden – such as a wall or fence.

▷ As the work progresses, your garden will start to look less like a battlefield and your design will begin to take shape.

▽ A loaded wheelbarrow can destroy a lawn if you make repeated trips, so create a temporary path.

Sorting out the sub-base

ONCE YOU'VE dug out the foundation area you'll need to lay the sub-base, which is the materials used to fill the excavated area.

Choosing your ingredients

There are many 'recipes' for sub-bases, but for solid paving that will carry frequent foot traffic, it's best to take a safe option. Excavate to a depth of 150mm plus the thickness of your paving, then lay 100mm of crushed, compacted hardcore and top it with 50mm of either concrete (for paving slabs) or sharp sand (for bricks and setts). Note that, in the case of hardcore and sand, these are compacted depths. Allow for a little compression, or you may find you need to top up your levels and compact again – though this is easy enough.

Estimating materials for concrete

Calculate the size of your patio in square metres and cross-reference to work out the required quantities of gravel, sand and cement needed for a 50mm layer of concrete. A bag of sand, cement or gravel is often roughly 25kg, but this will vary with water content – 1000kg is equal to one tonne.

Area of patio (square metres)	Materials required (kilograms)		
	Gravel	Sharp sand	Cement
1	60	30	15
2	120	60	30
3	180	90	45
4	240	120	60
5	300	150	75
6	360	180	90
7	420	210	105
8	480	240	120
9	540	270	135
10	600	300	150
11	660	330	165
12	720	360	180
13	780	390	195
14	840	420	210
15	900	450	225
16	960	480	240
17	1020	510	255
18	1080	540	270
19	1140	570	285
20	1200	600	300

Mechanical advantage

If you are mixing your own concrete, then a petrol- or electric-powered mixer is invaluable and shouldn't cost too much to hire for a weekend. To make the concrete, mix cement, sand and gravel in a ratio of 1:2:4 and add a little water, so it's wet but not runny. Mix up batches large enough to cover no more than 3m² at a time, or the concrete will begin to harden before you have a chance to use it.

How much will I need?

SUPPLIERS OFTEN offer liquid, ready-to-use concrete by the cubic metre – which makes working out your required quantities easy – but you are much more likely to have to order hardcore and sand by the tonne. If this is the case, a tonne of hardcore will cover about 5m² when

CAUTION: WORKING WITH CONCRETE

Cement (and, as a result, concrete) is a dangerous substance that can cause serious skin damage. Always wear gloves when handling it.

compacted to 100mm, and a tonne of sand will cover around 10m² at a thickness of 50mm. Okay, if you don't want to do the maths yourself, a cubic metre of concrete will cover 20m² at a thickness of 50mm. Ready-to-use concrete is, of course, delivered all at once (usually just poured at the roadside), and needs to be used before it sets.

▼ **If access is tricky and you need to move materials by hand, think about the logistics before the delivery lorry arrives!**

Mixing your own

For smaller projects it would be cheaper and more convenient to buy the cement, sand and gravel and mix up your own concrete as required. To calculate the quantities you will need, work out the area of your paving in square metres and multiply this by 15, 30 and 60 respectively to get the required weights of cement, sharp sand (see glossary, page 160) and gravel in kilograms (see Estimating Materials for Concrete, page 48). For example, if your patio measures 2m by 3m, then its area is 6m², and so you will need 90kg of cement, 180kg of sharp sand and 360kg of gravel.

Cost vs. convenience

Another option is to buy ready-mixed, or 'all in', concrete (a mixture of cement, gravel and sand) to which you add water. This saves time compared with mixing your own and is a good idea if you lack confidence in calculating quantities, but it can work out considerably more expensive.

Working out quantities for a sub-base

Weights are given in kilograms. Cross reference the area of your patio with the desired compacted depth of gravel or sand to work out how much you will need.

Area of patio (square metres)	Compacted depth of material (millimetres)			
	50	75	100	150
1	100	150	200	300
2	200	300	400	600
3	300	450	600	900
4	400	600	800	1200
5	500	750	1000	1500
6	600	900	1200	1800
7	700	1050	1400	2100
8	800	1200	1600	2400
9	900	1350	1800	2700
10	1000	1500	2000	3000
11	1100	1650	2200	3300
12	1200	1800	2400	3600
13	1300	1950	2600	3900
14	1400	2100	2800	4200
15	1500	2250	3000	4500
16	1600	2400	3200	4800
17	1700	2550	3400	5100
18	1800	2700	3600	5400
19	1900	2850	3800	5700
20	2000	3000	4000	6000

Excavating a foundation

THIS IS the most physical part of any paving work, so don't be too shy to ask friends for help. You'll need marker posts for this job – there are instructions on how to make these on page 43.

1 MARK out the area to be paved using pegs and string. If you are building a stone or slab patio, you will need to dry–lay (see page 62) once you have done this. Remove the turf and topsoil to an initial depth of 150mm within this area **A**.

2 USING a club hammer, drive a row of marker posts into the ground every 1.5m **B**, until the tops are flush with the desired final level of the paving. If your paving adjoins a building, make sure the post tops are at least 150mm below the building's damp–proof course.

A

B

3 USING a straight edge, a spirit level and a suitable shim, work across the excavated area, knocking each row of pegs deeper (see table, page 44) to create the appropriate fall **C**.

4 USING a spade – and a trowel where necessary – remove any excess soil until the lowest mark on each of your posts is showing; this will be the bottom of the lowest layer of the foundation **D**. Finally, compact the soil, using a plate compactor, roller or up–ended sledgehammer.

C

D

A sub-base for paving slabs

Paving slabs, which can be constructed from either natural or reconstituted stone, are best laid directly onto a bed of wet concrete, so that they are supported evenly. For instructions on mixing concrete see pages 48–50.

1 Having dry-laid the paving (see page 62) and excavated the area required (see previous page), throw on crushed hardcore (also known as type one) **A** and rake it evenly to the level of the second line on your marker posts (see page 42).

2 Compact the hardcore very thoroughly, using a garden roller, an up-ended sledgehammer or (best of all) a plate compactor **B**. Check that the compaction hasn't pushed the hardcore below the required level; if it has you will need to top up and compact again.

3 When the hardcore is completely solid, cover it with a thin layer of sharp sand – called a blinding layer – to fill any holes or gaps **C**. Compact the foundations again, then avoid walking on them unnecessarily. Prepare your paving materials before continuing with the work.

4 Before you mix your concrete, turn to pages 62–66 to find out how to lay your paving, as you will need to place the slabs while the concrete is still wet. Mix your concrete **D** and lay it in batches covering no more than 3m², filling to the top mark on your posts. Pull up the marker posts as you go, filling the holes with sand.

A sub-base for bricks and setts

SMALLER PAVING elements such as bricks or stone setts can create a warm and informal look. Less prone to cracking or shifting, they can be laid with mortar onto a bed of sand.

1 USING timber boards – pressure-treated to resist rot – create a retaining edge around the excavated area **A**, holding the boards firmly in place with timber posts. (Alternatively, you may wish to build a boundary of edging or kerb-stones set in concrete on a bed of hardcore.)

2 WITH the marker posts in place (see page 42), rake out hardcore **B** to the level of the second mark. This should give you a base layer 100mm thick. Compact it with a plate compactor, and check the level against your marker posts, topping up as needed.

3 NEXT, throw a layer of sand on top of the layer of hardcore **C** (note that a blinding layer to fill any gaps in the hardcore isn't strictly necessary) and then compact it down. Once you have done this, you need to add a second layer of sand and compact again.

4 PULL up the marker posts as you go, filling the holes with sand **D**. Sand is a soft material, so make sure nobody walks across it before you lay your paving. If you are unable to put the paving down immediately, cover the sub-base with a tarpaulin.

Building your patio

THE ADDITION of a patio can transform the way you use your garden, so it is worth putting time and effort into building it. Give some serious thought to the choice of paving material too, as this will affect the feel and layout of the project.

Material options

LOOSE STONES or wood chips are the quickest and easiest surfaces to lay, though they are not particularly long lasting and require frequent maintenance. At the other end of the scale, large, smooth paving slabs or stones, while being more difficult to lay, will make an impression and are great for paving a large area with straight edges. For a more homely, rustic effect, on the other hand, it's hard to beat traditional bricks and

▼ **Put the work into creating your patio, and you will have a wonderful place to relax and entertain friends on a sunny afternoon.**

Top tip

Before you make your final choice of materials, walk around the site and make a mental note of the surfaces and textures already in place. Mixing lots of different elements can be fun but often leads to a messy-looking whole. You are on safer ground if you match your new installation to the surrounding area.

setts – and these are also much easier to lay in curving patterns. Finally, you may wish to consider surfacing your patio with concrete. It's a surprisingly versatile substance that can create a wide range of interesting effects.

▲ It's important for your patio to have good views across the garden – if the weather's fine, you'll be spending a lot of time there.

▼ Your choice of materials is almost unlimited, but take your time and choose something that will fit in with the rest of your property.

Planning your patio

- Remember that the most common use for a patio is to entertain friends and family – don't situate yours too far from the kitchen or you'll find yourself running back and forth the whole time.

- Consider the view from your patio across the rest of the garden if you really want to make the most of your space. Would you prefer to have an enclosed, secluded courtyard effect, or an open area with a glorious vista – perhaps taking in lots of flowering borders?

- Perhaps the most common cause for regret after building a patio is simply that it is not bigger. If in doubt, adding a few square metres is a good idea – and won't add much to your construction costs.

- A large area of paving will soak up heat from the sun during the day and release it at night, creating a favourable microclimate for you, your guests and your tender plants. Consider improving on this by building trellis panels or screens to block out the wind.

- Store any leftover slabs or setts safely, in case you need them to make repairs in the future.

Loose-aggregate patios

STONE CHIPPINGS, gravel or even shredded bark or chipped wood can make excellent patio surfaces in the right situation, and offer low–cost (and low–effort) alternatives. With so much less weight pressing down on the ground it is usually not even necessary to lay foundations in any real sense. Remember, however, that these surfaces are not particularly long–term or maintenance-free – particularly around the edges, which can become untidy quite quickly. They may need regular weeding (particularly true of wood and bark) and sweeping back into place, as foot traffic causes the particles to move about.

Special qualities

Loose aggregates, as these materials are called, also have their own distinct advantages. For gravel and chipped stone, one of the most useful is their security value – anyone approaching your house along a gravel pathway or across an area of slate chippings will find it very hard to do so without making a noise. Wood chippings on the other hand are soft and yielding – perfect for places where kids will be playing.

▼ **The softening effect of a gravel patio can be enhanced with a loose arrangement of flowering plants in containers.**

Stone patios

STONE PROVIDES a stylish option for paving your patio. Large, smooth slabs of granite or sandstone will create a sense of cool, modern sophistication, while rougher slate or limestone, though still impressive, is rather less formal. This form of surface is best for strong patterns with straight edges, though you can tone down the geometry slightly by using a mixture of slab sizes to create a random pattern. Many paving companies offer kits with a number of different-sized elements to allow you to do just this.

The real thing?

There is a lot of snobbery about using real, or 'natural', stone, but you'd do well to ignore this if your budget is tight. Reconstituted stone and other artificial alternatives have come a long way in recent years, to the point where good

examples are hard to tell from the real thing. In fact, because they are more uniform in size and shape, they are often easier to lay. With the cost of fashionable natural-stone options such as travertine and slate rising year on year, the availability of good 'fakes' is sure to expand.

On the other hand, if budget is less of an issue, or if you wish to match a particular material already used in your house and garden, then there's no denying that quarried stone has its own special magic. If you ask them nicely, most retailers will supply you with a small sample of your chosen material to take away and try out at home.

▼ **Any project involves a certain amount of disruption to your home and garden while it's under way, but it will soon start to take shape.**

Paving with bricks

OR A relaxed, comfortable feel, a patio made from bricks or setts is an excellent option – particularly for anyone with a more traditional house and garden. If this idea appeals to you, consider one of the 'roll-out' paving systems now on offer. These essentially comprise a grid of plastic ties holding a number of small bricks in position, so you can lay a couple of square metres of paving at a stroke.

If you feel up to a bigger job, then paving with individual bricks is certainly worth the effort. It involves less heavy lifting than laying slab paving, and you may also find more opportunity for artistic expression. Not only can you choose between a number of laying patterns but you could also use more than one colour of brick to create a unique design.

Concrete patios

ALTHOUGH NOT perhaps the most obvious choice, it is perfectly possible to make an attractive patio out of concrete – particularly if you have a very modern home. If you talk to an expert at a good builders' merchant, he will probably surprise you with the range of options available, from rough, lava–like surfaces to incredibly polished finishes with gentle swirls of colour. Many leading architects are still fans of this versatile material, despite the bad press it has received after countless 1960s mistakes. Not something for the faint–hearted perhaps – but if, after you've tried it, you hate the way it looks, you will at least have an excellent surface to pave over!

Plants for patios

ONCE THE permanent structures of paths and paving are in place you can begin to add plants. Use herbs such as rosemary, thyme and mint around an entertaining area, and they will release their scent every time you brush past. You can even pick a few handfuls to throw on your barbecue.

As well as planting the beds and borders around your paving, you can use plants in containers – ideally finished with gravel or slate chippings to keep the compost in place. These will be a highly visible part of your design, so don't cut corners. Seek out pots that match the style of your garden and remember that plants will do best in larger containers.

▼ **The abrupt edges of hard landscaping can be softened most effectively with low-growing foliage.**

▲ A patio is an important (and well-used) destination in the garden, so think about how you will get there.

Accessing your patio

DON'T FORGET, when building your patio, that it is part of the wider garden and must relate to the other elements in the design. If you have an overall plan for your plot, then you may already have considered paths to and from the house, shed or conservatory, a rose–covered archway leading to the lawn, or a flower-filled planting wall dividing the patio from other beds and borders. Walls will act as dividers – separating one area from another – while paths will provide a means of access. An archway, particularly if filled with a gate or door, can be viewed as either; simply by opening or closing the door you can subtly influence the patio's atmosphere.

Building a gravel or wood-chip patio

A QUICK AND simple option for anyone who wants to make a patio in a hurry (or on a tight budget) is to dispense with building foundations and instead lay a loose aggregate such as gravel, shredded bark, wood chip or similar on top of a weed-excluding membrane.

1 MARK out the area of your patio with some pegs and string. Remove and dispose of the turf and topsoil to a depth of 50mm. Level the remaining earth as much as possible (using a spirit level and straight edge) **A** and tread it down until firm.

2 USING a club hammer, drive 30cm-long wooden posts into the ground at 1.5m intervals around the edge of the area. Then screw lengths of 50mm x 25mm treated timber to them to create a basic border. Check that the frame is level all around your excavation before you continue **B**.

3 LAY out on the ground either a sheet or a roll of water-permeable, light-excluding membrane – sometimes referred to as weed barrier or landscape fabric. If more than one sheet of membrane is required, overlap any edges by at least 30cm and hold in place with metal pins or tent pegs **C**.

4 FINALLY, cover the membrane with a 50mm layer of aggregate so that the timber edging is only just visible. You can either use gravel, pebbles, wood chip, bark or any other loose material that has an appearance you like. Rake this flat and tread it down firmly **D**.

Building a stone or slab patio

THE MOST popular option for garden patios has to be traditional rectangular paving slabs made of stone, reconstituted stone or concrete. These should be laid on a sub–base of crushed hardcore topped with concrete.

1 LAY your paving loosely on the ground in its final position **A** (known as 'dry–laying'), so you can check dimensions and make sure everything looks as it should. Start from a point of reference (such as a house wall) and work outwards.

2 MARK out, excavate and construct a sub–base **B** (see pages 51–52). Note that your slabs will be laid directly onto the concrete while it is still wet, so you will need to make sure you that you have them close to hand before you start mixing.

3 Mix and spread the concrete gradually **c**, covering about 3m² at a time. Starting in a corner – and against a

- boundary wall, if there is one in the plot
- – drop the mix into place with a spade
- then flatten it out with a trowel.

4 Wet the back of your first slab with a damp brush **D**, then lay it on to the concrete. Tap the slab down to the required

- level using a rubber mallet and then check
- the alignment in both directions with the
- aid of a spirit level.

5 WORKING from the corner, lay the first row across the site – following the direction of the slope (if there is one) – with 5mm spacers between each slab **E**. Check the levels as you lay, and tap down as necessary to maintain the required fall.

6 ONCE the first row is in place, lay the two adjoining edges **F** – to give three complete sides to the patio – then fill in the centre, working backwards from the first row. Check that each slab is level and that any fall is maintained.

7 WHEN all of the paving slabs are in place, leave them for around 48 hours before allowing anyone to walk on them. By then, the concrete will have set hard, so you can remove the spacers **G**, and fill the gaps between the slabs.

8 MIX up one part cement to three parts sand (with no water), and sweep this into the cracks between the slabs. Push the mixture down with the edge of a trowel **H**, and repeat. Gently dampen the patio with a fine spray and leave the cement to set.

How to cut slabs

UNLESS YOU'RE very lucky, there will come a point when you need to cut a slab down to size. How you go about this depends on your budget and whether you intend to do more paving in future.

Option 1

1 To cut a stone or concrete slab, rest it on a bed of sand, and draw the line of the cut onto the slab using a pencil and straight edge.

2 WEARING eye protection and gloves, use a brick bolster and club hammer to cut a groove along the pencil line **A**, gradually working deeper until the slab breaks in two.

Option 2

For a neater and easier cut, you could invest in an angle grinder with a stone-cutting disc **B**. In this case, you should wear a particle mask and ear defenders as well as gloves and eye protection.

Building a patio from bricks or setts

THIS METHOD works very well for bricks or for small setts. If you are using large or unevenly shaped setts, lay them in generous amounts of mortar (placed directly on the sub-base in batches of 3m²), leave to dry for 48 hours and then sweep with fine sand.

1 FIRST mark out, excavate **A** and construct a sub-base (see pages 51 and 53). Because sand will move if you tread on it, you should be careful not to walk over the sub-base too much before you lay your paving.

2 SPREAD out a 15mm thick layer of uncompacted sharp sand – which is also known as screed – over the sub-base, and level it off with a long straight edge **B**.

3 WORKING from several packs at a time (to mix up any variations in colour), start laying your paving along the longest retaining edge – or the bottom of a slope, if there is one. Push the bricks into the sand, working across the patio **C**.

4 WHEN you reach the edges and corners of your patio, cut the bricks to fit (see page 68). If you have a lot of cutting to do then a special block cutter is very useful **D**. When you have finished laying the bricks, run across the patio two or three times with a plate compactor, to settle the paving firmly into place.

5 BRUSH fine kiln–dried sand across the paving so that it fills the joints. Run across the patio again with the compactor to shake the sand downwards, then sweep in more sand **E**. Compact again until there are no more gaps. This is a much easier job if the weather, and in particular the surface of the block paving, is as dry as possible. The setts will stay in place perfectly well if you need to put this last step off for a few days.

How to cut bricks

TO CUT bricks, use a bolster to score all the way around, then place the brick on a firm surface (with the indented side downwards), hold the bolster on the line of the cut and strike firmly. You can also use a brick hammer (which has a strong chisel–like end) to chip small pieces off the brick.

Traditional patterns

THERE ARE many traditional bricklaying patterns, each with its own particular character. Stack is the simplest option and has a modern–looking design. Running bond is elegant and is also easy to lay. Basketweave (which is also known as parquet) is a very striking pattern, while the sectional design, consisting of blocks of paving with alternating patterns, works best over larger areas. The concentric pattern, with the gaps filled in with gravel, is great for informal patios. Herringbone pattern is very stylish, but the edging can be difficult.

Running bond

Basketweave

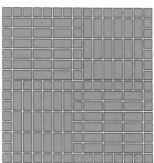

Sectional

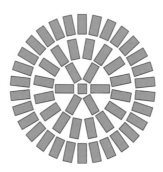

Concentric

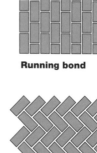

Herringbone

Stack

Timber decking

THE LAST decade has seen a huge surge in the number of people choosing to install timber decking, and, though that popularity has perhaps dropped off a little recently (no doubt as a result of overexposure), there are many situations where a deck is very much the perfect solution.

A host of qualities

ONE OBVIOUS advantage is that the physical effort involved in building decking is much less than for stone paving – many people feel more comfortable attempting a job that doesn't involve much mixing of concrete and mortar, not to mention digging out extensive foundations. A deck is an easy way to overcome difficulties arising from a sloping or uneven site, and the natural appearance of timber can feel warm and inviting. There are few materials that work better with water than wood; the clean, formal lines of the decking counterbalancing the changeable nature of a pool or fountain. A slight overhang at the edge of a deck is one of the easiest and most attractive ways to conceal an untidy pond edge, and a wooden walkway can give comfortable access to the most marshy and wild of bog gardens.

Cost considerations

Building a deck is also a comparatively low–cost way of landscaping an area, and timber will stand up to years of abuse if you give it just a little regular maintenance. As with any project, this is not to say that you should skimp on the budget. Cheap materials can lead to a cheap-looking result, so go for the best timber and fixings you can afford.

▼ **You can create a self-contained garden 'room' for yourself with an expanse of deck and some clever borders.**

▲ **Decking is a hugely versatile material – able to fit into unusual shapes and cope well with changes of level.**

Top tip

Changes in level add visual interest to an area of decking, particularly in an otherwise flat garden. As a point of safety, bring attention to the change in level by setting the bottom of the facing board (or riser) of the step slightly above the ground. The shadow created beneath it will be more noticeable than a simple join between two wooden surfaces.

Before starting

THE PLACEMENT and design of a deck are crucial to its success so, as with all large projects, it pays to take your time at the design stage. Consider how you will use the deck and how often – if it's mostly for entertaining, is it close enough to the kitchen, and is there a direct route between the two? If you have private relaxation in mind, can the site be overlooked by neighbours or passers–by? If it's only for occasional use, does it disrupt your view of the garden from the house? Apart from these considerations, there is the more basic aspect of exposure to the elements. Take a few days to observe how long – and at what times – the site is in the sun and how you will shelter it from the wind. A little patience now will pay dividends.

Work with the surroundings

Once you have decided on the location of the deck, you can then begin to think about its appearance. Though wood is a natural material, the look of decking is not organic. This allows you to play with the contrast between the clean lines of the deck and the more random form of the surrounding planting. Allow the two to intermingle by using creeping plants and

▲ Decking lends itself to simplicity, but that can include the introduction of interesting twists and curves in the design.

Top tip

Location is the most important aspect of deck design – get this right and the rest will fall into place.

overhanging branches, while any barren areas of deck can be softened with the addition of container–grown specimen plants.

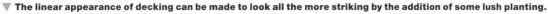

▼ The linear appearance of decking can be made to look all the more striking by the addition of some lush planting.

Building your deck

THERE ARE two main ways of constructing decking. One is to build a frame of beams and suspend joists between them, so that the top edges of the beams and joists line up. This has the advantage of offering a shallow profile, which allows the surface to remain close to the surrounding ground or water level. This construction will be strong enough for most purposes and is the method used in the following step–by–steps. The other option is to lay the joists across (i.e. on top of) the frame of beams – stronger and easier to build, but it will be up to twice as deep.

Top tips

Use balustrades to define edges and protect flowerbeds. Any railings around water need to be solidly built.

Built-in bench seating will add a further dimension and be easy to maintain, but too much will cut down on space.

▼ **The clean lines and linear appearance of timber decking will frequently suit a modern building.**

Surface finish

Once the frame has been constructed, you can begin to place the decking boards – a simple task whichever construction of joists and beams you choose. Decking boards are available with a number of finishes, but the most common is a reversible board featuring one smooth side and one with pre–cut grooves. This detailing can be used to give extra grip, but, if the decking is likely to become slippery (i.e. if it is close to water), you would still do better to cover the boards with wire mesh. The grooves do give the deck an interesting look, but they also make it more difficult to clean.

Tricking the eye

Either way, the direction in which you lay the boards has an important role to play. If you have a long, narrow garden, position the boards perpendicular to the length of the garden, drawing the eye sideways and making the garden seem wider. If the garden is short (or the deck is small) running the boards away from the

observer will appear to lengthen the deck and the garden beyond. This simple trick has been used for centuries by painters, architects and fashion designers.

A twist on this theme can be used to enliven a deck walkway or path. Believe it or not, running the boards along the length of the path will cause people to walk along it quickly, while paths made up of boards that cross them will encourage a more relaxed pace with frequent stops to look around. When a path changes direction, a change in the direction of the boarding is a nice touch.

Decking design considerations

- For a rustic feel, allow boards to finish at different lengths, giving a staggered edge. Using round wood for the rails adds to this affect.

- If you use decking close to water, keep fountains and other features a safe distance away. Constant splashing will result in the build-up of unsightly algae.

- To add variety to an expanse of deck, consider varying the direction of the boards to create a chequered pattern.

- Contrast is a valuable tool. The sharp boundaries that occur when you place wood next to water, stone or soil can give a cool, contemporary feel.

- Where the edges of a deck appear too harsh, they can be softened using round stones or low, creeping plants.

- A very modern and clean look can be created with multiple levels, overhangs and changes in direction.

- A wooden walkway, raised on solid timber posts, is a great way to grant access to boggy parts of the garden.

- To make a path appear longer, run the boards lengthways down it. For a feeling of width, run them across the path.

▲ **Timber decking works well with water, providing a clever way of disguising the unsightly edges of ponds.**

▼ **Where decking changes in level, ballustrading is a wise addition and steps may be a necessity.**

Adding rails

MANY DIY stores and mail–order retailers now offer timber railings – or balustrades – to add the finishing touch to your deck. They usually come as a kit, comprising main structural uprights, base rails, handrails and decorative balusters.

Think ahead

If you know from the start that you want to have a balustrade around your deck, then you should fix the main uprights to the subframe of the deck before laying the decking boards. You can cut notches out of the boards to lay them around these uprights before putting the base rail,

◀ **A sloping site offers the opportunity to create space beneath a deck that can be used for discrete storage.**

▼ **A patio built flat on the ground can be broken up with other materials – such as boulders and plants.**

CAUTION: USING A JIGSAW

- As with any power tool, it is important to use ear defenders and goggles when using a jigsaw.

- Remove any loose clothing that could get caught in the jigsaw.

- Make sure the work piece is firmly supported so that it does not move during the operation.

- Make sure the cable will allow the jigsaw to move without dragging and that it will not come near the blade while you are working.

- Allow the machine to come to a rest before trying to draw out the blade.

▶ **Planting is an important part of dressing up your deck, and a planting hole such as this one is much lower maintenance than growing in a container. Not only can the plant put down deeper roots (so requiring less watering) but there is also no problem with pots staining the wood green with algae.**

handrail and balusters in place. Note that the positioning of the balustrade supports may influence the spacing of deck supports of a raised deck because they can't both be right in the corner of the frame. The balustrade supports should therefore be in the corner, as they are going to be visible and should look 'right' to the eye. The decking support will easily hold up a corner of decking that is cantilevered slightly beyond it.

Anatomy of a jigsaw

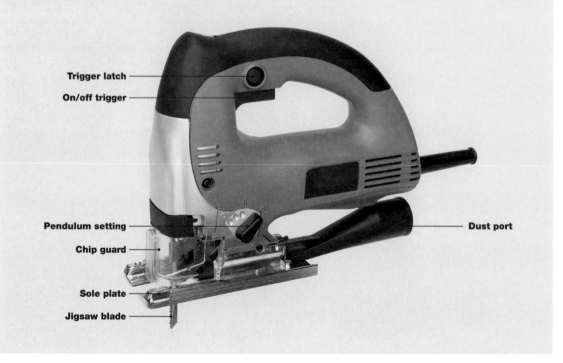

Trigger latch

On/off trigger

Pendulum setting

Chip guard

Sole plate

Jigsaw blade

Dust port

Building a simple deck

THE CONSTRUCTION of a deck on flat, level ground is a straightforward project – ideal for any DIY novice – and a great way to create an outdoor entertaining space on a small budget.

1 MARK out the position of your deck and bang in timber pegs to mark the corners. Use a tape measure and a builder's square if you have one **A**. If you don't, just measure the diagonals to make sure they are equal.

2 CLEAR the ground of any plants, weeds or grass, lifting the whole layer of turf including the roots. Use a long straight edge and a spirit level to check the ground doesn't slope **B**, and use a spade and rake to level the earth where required.

Coach screws

For strong joins in structural timber (such as between the support posts and beams of a timber deck) a good choice of fixing is the coach screw. These tend to be longer and thicker than a normal screw, though still with the same spiralling thread. Their size means they are harder to drive into the wood so, instead of a slotted or 'Phillips' head, they have hexagonal heads like bolts. Use a socket wrench instead of a screwdriver to twist them into place, or fit your electric drill/screwdriver with a socket bit. You'll probably need to pre-drill the holes too.

3 IF the deck is on damp ground, dig a hole (150mm square and 150mm deep) every 1.2m across the area in both directions. Fill with quick-drying concrete to 30mm above ground level, and check the top surfaces are flat and level **C**.

4 TREAD the ground until solid and cover with water-permeable, weed-proof membrane to prevent anything growing back – cutting holes for the concrete pads if required. Overlap any edges between the sheets of membrane by at least 300mm then top with a 40mm layer of gravel **D**.

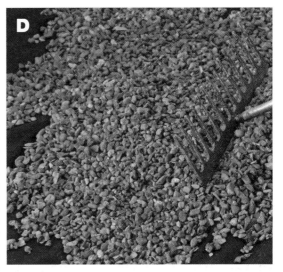

5 To assemble the subframe, lay out the outer frame and fix with two coach screws at each corner. You will need to pre-drill and countersink each hole. Place the inner joists at 400mm intervals (centre to centre), and fix in the same way **E**.

6 FIX the boards to every joist using two decking screws **F**. Allow a 3mm gap between each board for drainage and expansion. Paint any cut ends with an end-grain preserver.

Building supports for a raised deck

IF YOUR deck runs across an uneven or sloping site you'll need to install timber 'legs' to carry it. This is not a difficult job, but it will give your project a real air of professionalism.

1 MARK out and clear the area of the proposed deck of any turf or weeds **A** and bang in timber pegs to mark the corners. Use a surveyor's tape measure and a builder's square if you have one. If you don't, just measure the diagonals to make sure they are equal. Your support posts should be no more than 1.2m apart.

2 DIG a hole for each support post that is approximately 600mm deep and 300mm wide **B**. If you can, widen the bottom with a trowel so the foundation ends up being slightly cone shaped.

3 PLACE each post in its hole and use a spirit level to make sure it's vertical. Pour in quick–setting concrete **C** and allow at least two full days for this to set before continuing.

4 TREAD the ground between the posts until it's solid, then cover it with weed–proof, water–permeable membrane **D**. Overlap any edges between sheets of membrane by 300mm then top with 40mm of gravel.

5 Fix the edges of the subframe onto the outsides of the support posts with coach screws. Install the other frame elements **E** and the decking boards just as in steps 5 and 6 of the previous project.

6 Skirt the edge of the deck with trellis panels to conceal the void underneath. These panels can be screwed directly to the subframe or support posts **F**.

Surveyor's tape measure

Standard metal tape measures are great over short distances, but on the larger scale of a garden you'll probably need something a little longer. A surveyor's tape measure is just the thing, and it won't break the bank. Typically available in lengths of 25, 30 or 50m, this tape will allow you to accurately measure the length and width of the whole garden. Don't forget that the tape is not rigid, so it has to be held taught to give the correct measurement.

Adding rails and balustrades

AVOID THE risk of accidents by edging your decking with timber balustrades wherever there is a change in level. Balustrades also look attractive near water and provide the perfect spot to lean and enjoy a chilled glass of wine.

1 IF you're including a rail in your design, fix its structural posts to the subframe of the deck before you put down the boards **A**. In this design, space has been left between the deck supports and the outside of the frame to allow the balustrade support to be fixed right in the corner.

2 LAY the decking boards across the subframe, fixing them onto each beam using two decking screws and allowing 3mm between adjoining boards. At the point where the boards run into the balustrade support, mark out a square of timber with the same dimensions as the support and cut out with a jigsaw. Then fit the board around the balustrade **B**.

3 CUT the base rails and handrails to length, so that they fit between the supports (a maximum of 1.2m gives plenty of strength). Drill pilot holes to prevent splitting, then screw the balusters into the underside of the handrail, and through from the underside of the base **C**.

4 USING a 12mm drill bit, drill two holes into both ends of each base rail and handrail. Insert 12mm dowels into each of these holes, and use them to help mark out and drill matching holes in the sides of the supports. Lift the railings into place and glue in the dowels **D**.

Cutting out planting holes

YOU CAN make a simple deck look a lot more interesting by creating a hole in the boards through which you can plant a tree or bush. This is a relatively simple procedure that will also allow you to save any existing plants in your garden that would otherwise have to be removed before the deck could be installed.

1 MARK out the edges of the hole using a soft pencil **A** and remove completely any decking boards that are marked in the process.

2 INSERT extra joists, perpendicular to those already in place, to create an area of subframe. Then, fix them in place, using two screws at each end **B**.

3 CUT the original boards to length using a handsaw. Some may need to be 'notched out' to fit around the hole. Use a jigsaw for this **C**.

4 IT might be easier to plant through the opening before rebuilding the deck, but once this is done, fix the boards back down around the hole **D**.

Paths

IT'S VERY easy to think of paths as the last thing you should add to your garden plan, but they are, in fact, one of the most visible parts of the design and well worth making a feature of. With a little creativity, you can use them to lead people on a tour of the garden, taking in the best views and experiences one after the other. This is a trick that landscape architects have used in the grounds of stately homes for centuries, but it can also work in your back garden.

▶ **Paths are crucial to effective garden design but, as always, think about the look of your existing garden when choosing materials.**

▼ **The simplest of designs, using irregularly shaped stones, can work beautifully in an informal scheme.**

Material considerations

THE MATERIALS that you choose are very important. Often just the smallest decorative touch is enough to remind you of a feature in another part of the garden, leaving you with a sense of satisfaction that only comes with really clever design. Imagine walking out of a house and crossing over a small sun terrace of quarry tiles, edged in a soft red brick, then wandering through the garden on a tiled path to come across a circular raised pond, the walls of which are made of the same red brick. You might not realize why you like that garden – just that it seemed to fit together.

Planning the route

DESIGNERS AND architects refer to the routes people most often take across an open space as 'desire lines'. These routes are influenced by a number of factors – from the very obvious, such as where people are coming from and going to, to the more obscure, such as shelter from the weather or interest in a particular plant. Your job when planning a garden is to predict where the desire lines will be and provide suitable paving. Remember that people don't like to waste energy – you can't expect them to trek around two sides of a garden when they can easily walk across the diagonal. This is why you often see muddy areas where public footpaths turn sharply; pedestrians simply cut the corner because the planners didn't interpret the desire lines correctly.

Well-trodden

If you are installing a path into an existing design (i.e. a garden that is already fairly well-established) then you may well be able to see these routes in the quality of the turf. Is there, for instance, a corner that always gets worn down, or a line across the middle of the lawn where the grass is getting thin? If so, this is a helpful indication of the places where you should think of laying your paving.

A fresh start

On the other hand, if your garden is a blank canvas – and your design exists only on paper – you will have to use your imagination to decide where your paths will run. The general rule is that people will take the most direct route from one place to another. While it is temporarily possible to persuade people to take a more indirect route – past some scented plants or a pretty pond, for example – this will soon grow familiar, and they will eventually revert to walking straight across the lawn. The only sure-fire way to force people to take any route other than the direct one is to physically block their other means of access with planting, trellises or some other obstruction.

▼ **Brick pavers are one of the most traditional materials for paths – perfectly suited to this cottage-style garden.**

◀ **This unusual combination of textures and colours is used here to heighten the interest and visual appeal of a serpentine path.**

to fit together). It is also likely to be the most cost–effective method, as buying in bulk is often cheaper and reduces wastage.

Clever combinations

Perhaps a more interesting option – though technically more challenging – is to use two different elements but combine them throughout the scheme rather than restrict them to their own part of the garden. For example, an elegant, pale, limestone paving slab can be used for a patio and major paths, while a darker stone sett could be used to edge these areas and perhaps make up a secondary patio.

You can create a sense of diversity, but still save money through bulk buying, by using a material in two different ways. For example, brick paving can be laid perpendicular to the house for main areas of paving but on the diagonal for edging or smaller paths. Paving suppliers are generally aware that people will want to do this kind of thing, and they have developed their product ranges with complementary elements to help. Whichever materials you opt for, keep in mind the overall look of the garden, and consider matching your style to that of existing elements, such as the house walls.

Choosing your style

WHEN LAYING a garden path, your options are similar to those described in the previous chapters on patios and decking. Some of the construction methods and materials are readily transferable, though you do need to consider the fact that paths are for movement, whereas patios and decks are generally for relaxation. While less–well–used paths will work perfectly well if made from gravel or wood chip, for areas of more regular traffic you might prefer to use something more substantial, such as brick or stone.

The simple route

There are as many styles of path as there are of patios and decks. If you are installing several areas of paving at once (perhaps a patio by the house, a couple of paths and a smaller seating area further down the garden), then the obvious choice is to use similar materials throughout to give a sense of continuity. This will probably be easier than combining several different types of paving, as it avoids the problem of joining one element to another (not all materials are designed

▶ **An effective technique is to create a 'destination' for a path using a focal point such as a piece of sculpture or a water feature.**

▲ **Stepping stones provide an attractive way to cross water, but the surfaces must be rough to avoid slipping.**

Stepping stones

THOUGH NOT frequently used, stepping stones provide an easy, low–cost way to create a short route across a lawn or area of planting. They will not stand up to heavy traffic, but are a great solution in places where you need only occasional access – or where a more substantial construction would ruin the look of the wider environment. If your garden is designed around an informal theme, is at all wooded or has a fairytale feel to it, then stepping stones will fit right in. You will obviously make considerable savings on the quantity of materials you need to buy, and it takes comparatively little work to lay them.

A simple task

As you are likely to be laying each of the paving elements singly (i.e. each slab on its own), rather than in a large mass, you don't really need to worry too much about stress fractures or movement. For this reason, your foundations can be considerably less substantial than is required for slabs or bricks. Simply cut away the turf and a little of the subsoil, line the hole with 50mm of sand and bed the slab firmly down on top so it is flush with the surrounding ground. On a very damp or unstable site, you may prefer to use a small sub–base of hardcore and concrete (see page 48), but this is an easy job on such a small scale. Should one of your stones develop a wobble, it is not difficult to lift it and re–lay.

Top tip

Stepping stones should be placed a comfortable walking stride apart. Once you know where you want your path, walk the route, and, at each step, place a tent peg in the ground next to the centre of the arch of your foot. This is where you should place the centre of the stepping stone.

Dual texture

The main drawback of stepping stones is that you are relying on people to step only on the stones – if they don't, you are likely to find the grass between them quickly becomes worn. For the same reason a stepping–stone path isn't suitable if you need to push a wheelbarrow along the route. A more hard–wearing alternative would be to create a gravel path with individual stone slabs laid regularly along it, allowing people the pleasure of experiencing the two textures combined.

▼ **Stepping stones, such as these ornamental log-effect pads, are a good idea for lightly trafficked routes.**

Making a path from gravel

THIS IS a low-effort, low-cost method of creating a path that won't have to carry much traffic. This particular path is made from gravel, but you can use other forms of loose aggregate. Start by marking out both sides of the path using pegs and string and removing the turf and topsoil to a depth of between 50 and 70mm within this area.

1 USE 70mm-wide pressure-treated timber boards and 50mm-square posts to create a solid retaining edge along each side of the excavation. Lay the boards in place first, then hammer in 450mm-long posts **A** and screw the boards to them.

2 TREAD the soil firmly down and lay a water-permeable, weed-excluding membrane **B**. This will allow rain to pass through without pooling along the path, but should prevent most weeds from growing through.

3 MAKE sure the edges of the membrane run up the insides of the timber **C**. Some membranes come on a handy roll around 900mm wide, which is a standard width for paths.

4 POUR the gravel onto the membrane **D** and spread it evenly along the path using a rake. Tread the material down thoroughly and ensure you have created a layer at least 50mm thick to prevent light reaching the soil beneath.

Laying a brick or sett path

PATHS MADE of small pavers such as bricks can look stunning. They can be laid into sharp sand on a shallow sub-base, but, seeing as they are not fixed in place, they must have solid retaining edges. You can make these edges with shaped edging stones bedded into mortar or more simply from pressure-treated timber.

1 MARK out the route of the path with pegs and string, and remove the turf and topsoil within this area to a depth of 100mm plus the depth of the pavers (around 65mm for a typical brick) **A**. Tread down the remaining soil as much as possible.

2 LAY a 75mm layer of crushed hardcore all along the path, and compact thoroughly with a plate compacter or an up-ended sledgehammer **B**. Bed the edging materials into mortar along both sides of the path and leave to set.

3 SPREAD 20mm of sharp sand over the hardcore **C** and compact by tamping down with a piece of timber the same width as the path – working from one end of the path to the other. On top of this spread 5mm of uncompacted soft sand.

4 FOLLOWING your chosen pattern (see page 68), lay the bricks tightly together onto the soft sand, tamping them down gently as you go. If any bed down too deeply, lift them and adjust the sand layer. Finally, brush soft sand over the whole path **D**.

Edging

DGING A patio can perhaps be thought of as a finishing touch – it's a nice way to define an area and can help prevent soil, gravel or other materials from intruding on your paving where it adjoins beds or borders. You may prefer to install edging at the same time as you build your patio, saving yourself extra effort mixing and laying concrete. Alternatively, if you'd prefer to lay the paving first and add the edging later (perhaps because funds will only stretch so far, or you don't have time to do both in one weekend), you can. Just be sure to keep the edges neat when building the sub–base for your patio – otherwise any overspill will set hard and obstruct your ongoing work.

Strong and tidy

OR PATHS, however, edging is perhaps more than just a design choice – it also adds strength to the structure, which may have to carry a heavy load over a small area. The edges

▲ **Edging can also have practical uses, such as containing loose materials around plantings beside paths and patios.**

of a path are also much more prominent (simply because paths are usually long and narrow) so tidying them up with an attractive border would really be worth the effort.

▼ **From an aesthetic point of view, edging is useful for providing a clear distinction between different parts of the garden.**

◀ **Edging is very good for keeping things neat and tidy, making a clear visual delineation between garden plants and a patio.**

level. If this step was made of the same materials as the rest of the installation, it could be difficult to spot, inviting accidents. Edge both parts of the patio in a contrasting stone – and extend this edging along the lip of the step – and you will create a warning of the change in level.

Deck edge options

When it comes to edging decking, you will find your choices are more limited. Any raised construction (or ones near water) should always be ringed with balustrades for safety reasons. This is an attractive feature in its own right.

Ground–level decks can certainly be left without edging – the contrast between timber and soil or stone being so strong. If you prefer (or you need to exclude soil or loose aggregates) you can use a low timber border, or simply construct the deck with a finished surface level 150–200mm above the ground.

Changing levels

The border of a path or patio can take many forms and will usually be either flush with the surrounding surfaces (ideal for visual emphasis, perhaps where a patio meets a lawn) or raised a little above them (the best option if you need to retain loose materials such as gravel or earth). A third option is to highlight the boundary still further by creating a low wall, raised planter or simple bench seating. This is perhaps not feasible down both sides of a long path but can add a great deal of interest around one or two sides of an otherwise flat patio.

Signalling change

Another useful feature of edging is that it creates a visual break between two surfaces, to alert people to a change in texture, level or direction. For example, if your patio is built across a sloping site, it may be necessary to have a long step across it, dividing the paving into an upper and lower

▶ **A strong edge allows you to mow the lawn right up to the path, avoiding unsightly, overgrown grass.**

While a path or patio is a tremendous asset to a garden in itself, adding improvements – even if it's just some garden furniture or a few fresh plants – can really make a difference. Water, in a pond or fountain, can add a sense of movement and magic to your garden, while low walls and steps can add interest, creating levels and dividing up the space. To extend the enjoyment of your garden into the evening, install some simple lights. The dramatic effects will far outweigh the work involved.

Additions & Improvements

Walls

Hard landscaping is not a two-dimensional art, and the most dramatic and effective garden designs will invariably make use of vertical surfaces and changes in ground level. Walls can be used in the garden for practical purposes, such as shelter and security, but also as a design element – breaking the space into smaller components and allowing you to vary the style and atmosphere in each separate area. The visual impact of a wall can also be used to create a backdrop to a planting arrangement or even to screen one part of the garden from view, providing a sense both of secrecy and anticipation. Your choice of material is limited only by your imagination – you can build a wall out of anything from traditional brickwork or rendered blocks to railway sleepers, bamboo or even glass. The construction of brick or stone walling on a large scale can be complex, requiring professional skills, but anything up to about a metre in height can be attempted by a confident DIYer. As with all masonry, good foundations are key.

Basic brickwork

If you choose to build in brick, you'll need to think about the laying pattern you will use – from simple stretcher bond (where the bricks are laid end to end to create a cheap wall only as thick as the width of one brick) to English, Flemish or garden wall bond (where bricks are

▼ **Walls can define a space in the garden, create a route through it or give you a place to sit and relax.**

laid alternately along and across the wall to create attractive patterns and a more robust result, as thick as the length of one brick). Have a look at walls elsewhere and decide which style you like.

Mixing mortar

Laying bricks is a simple job if you prepare carefully and mark out your site well. Take your time and regularly check that your lines are straight and level. Use a mortar of one part ordinary Portland cement to one part hydrated lime to six parts builder's sand for a standard job, or a 2:1:8 mix of the same ingredients for a stronger result. Add only as much water to this as is required to give a stiff mix that falls cleanly off the spade.

Laying the bricks

Use a mason's trowel to make a sausage shape of mortar, slightly smaller than your bricks. Scoop this up on the trowel, and tip it into position on

▼ **A retaining wall combines elegantly with a small set of steps – simple but inviting.**

the footing. Flatten the sausage with the trowel, until it's about 20mm thick. Lay the first brick on top, using a spirit level to check it is horizontal. If your bricks have an indentation (called a frog) on one side, lay this facing upwards.

Trim away excess mortar – or top up any gaps – with the trowel. Make another bed of mortar as before, but, before laying the next brick on top, scrape mortar for the vertical joint onto one end of the second brick. Continue laying, and check to see that your line is level every four or five bricks.

Pointing

Finally, point the joints between the bricks in order to exclude rain and frost and to neaten the overall appearance of your wall. Before the bricks have set hard together, use a pointing trowel to even up the mortar between them. Ideally, the mortar should cut in below the upper brick and then slope slightly outwards to the edge of the lower brick. This is designed to encourage rain water to run down the wall, instead of pooling in the joints.

Four types of brick bond

While the pattern in which bricks are arranged in a path is almost entirely a matter of aesthetics, the pattern, or bonding, of bricks in a wall must distribute the load and provide stability as well as looking good. The bonds shown here are tried and tested.

Stretcher bond

Used for a single skin wall, this is the cheapest and easiest bond to lay. All of the bricks are laid lengthways with the vertical joints staggered. The ends of a straight wall have half–bricks to fill in the gaps.

English bond

Alternate courses of stretchers and headers give a very strong wall of double thickness. Bricks cut in half along their length (called queen closers) are used to fill out the ends and corners of the wall.

Flemish bond

Headers alternate with pairs of parallel stretchers to make up each course, with the courses being staggered to give a very attractive finish. Queen closers are used as in the English bond.

English garden wall bond

Another double thickness wall, with each course of headers being topped with three staggered courses of parallel stretchers. Not as strong as the English bond, but perhaps easier to lay.

Building a low wall

A LOW WALL is a great way to add height and structure to any garden design. You can use walls either as borders (to edge and define a patio) or as barriers (to create a sense of privacy and enclosure). They can even be used as seating, if wide enough.

1 MARK out, excavate and then lay the foundations for the wall **A**. A wall up to 1m high and one brick (215mm) thick will need foundations 225mm deep – half hardcore and half concrete – and 450mm wide.

2 WHEN the foundations have set, dry–lay your bricks to work out the pattern **B**, then lay the first two courses with frost–proof bricks, using a string line – or board and spirit level – to ensure you are working straight.

3 INSERT line pins into the mortar at each corner and stretch a taught line between them to give you a level to work against **C**. Then lay the upper courses, building up the corners first so they step down. This will make it easier to maintain your levels, as any errors will become cumulative and thus easier to spot. Move the line up as you complete each course.

4 WHEN the last course of brickwork is in place and pointed, top with a layer of damp–proof membrane (DPM) to stop rainwater penetrating the wall. Lastly, lay shaped bricks or coping stones on top, on a bed of mortar spread evenly on the DPM **D**.

Steps

ANY SIGNIFICANT change in ground level is much easier to navigate if you break it into a number of steps, but there is more involved here than purely practical concerns. Steps are an interesting combination of boundary and point of entrance, perhaps deserving of a frame of raised brick piers or a timber arch at the top or bottom. They are a particularly dramatic part of a garden design, and offer you the chance to create sharp contrasts, even in a small space. Since they are a relatively complex construction project, they should be considered early in the planning process.

Safety is an important consideration when designing a change in level – you may well wish to add lighting here, even if nowhere else in the garden, and the proportions and placement of the steps themselves should fall within accepted parameters. In some situations a balustrade or handrail will be required, and the surface materials should be non–slip in all weather conditions.

▼ **Where paths need to step up, be sure to highlight the alteration in level with a visible change in materials.**

Getting the height right

NOT ALL steps are alike in their dimensions and layout, but there is an accepted range that pedestrians will find safe and comfortable. Note that the shape of an interior stairway is not a good guide for external constructions, which need to be much less steep to allow for comfortable movement (and which rarely have handrails). The general rule is that as the height of each step increases, the width decreases.

The steepest flight should have risers (i.e. vertical faces) of 175mm and treads (horizontal surfaces) of 300mm. Shallow steps should be as wide as 450mm but no less than 110mm high, otherwise they can be difficult to negotiate. For some reason, most people find a flight of one or two steps in a path a little bit awkward to traverse – so aim for three steps as a minimum. Longer flights of stairs (in a steep garden, for instance) should have no more than 12 or 14 steps between 'landings', and you should also consider providing a handrail.

A split-level patio

IF YOUR garden has only a small change in level, you can most likely allow for this with gentle gradients in areas of lawn or planted beds. If you wish to pave over such an area, however, you will need either to flatten the soil completely (usually by digging away the higher part and spreading the spoil over the lower part) or to incorporate a change in level in the finished paving. This is easily accomplished, and will usually take the form of a single, long step across the width of the patio. The two halves don't have to be of equal size, but try not to build the step too close to one edge, as this can look like a mistake. Build the lower area of paving first, then lay the step along the edge adjoining the upper level. Allow a 150mm gap between the 'inside' or the back edge of the first tread and the outer edge of the patio – effectively you are using the sub-base of the patio to support the step, so you don't want to build right up to the boundary. Next, excavate the footing for the upper level and fill with hardcore and concrete up to the top of the step. The final job is to lay the paving for the upper patio – but it's a good idea to use a different-coloured material on the step itself to alert people to the change in level.

▲ Outdoors, changes in level can serve to create several discrete areas within the garden.

▼ At the entrance to a house, a simple set of two steps can create an interesting threshold, particularly if dressed with potted plants.

▲ Long flights of steps should be broken up by wider landings to allow people to rest on their way up.

◀ Whatever their purpose, steps should be of an even height and length to make walking up or down them safe and comfortable.

▲ Landscape architects often prefer a sloping site simply because there is so much more scope for interest in the design.

▼ The challenge of steps can be overcome in many ways, and they can become a feature in themselves.

Building brick- and-slab steps

A BASIC CONSTRUCTION combining brick risers with slabs for the treads is ideal for most short slopes in a garden setting. Match the materials to paving elsewhere in the garden.

1 WORK out the shape of the steps and cut this into the earth using a spade. At the bottom step, dig down 125mm and lay a sub-base of 25mm compacted hardcore topped with 100mm concrete. Level it out and leave for 72 hours.

2 AT the front edge of the sub-base, build a riser (see Basic Brickwork, page 96), using two courses of brick across the width of the step. Allow the mortar to set thoroughly then fill in behind the riser with hardcore and compact with a sledgehammer.

3 LAY your paving slabs on a bed of mortar on top of the first step, projecting the front edge over the bricks by 25mm and sloping the slab slightly forward for drainage. Allow the mortar to set, then point the joints with more mortar.

4 BUILD the next brick riser in the same way on the back edge of the first row of slabs and continue up the slope. The last tread in the flight of steps should finish flush with the surrounding ground.

Top tip

It is important to light up any steps in the garden, as they can be a trip hazard in the dark. Put down the wiring for any lights (see Anatomy of exterior wiring on page 118) before you lay your paving, otherwise you may have a difficult job later.

Building timber steps

A SIMPLE TIMBER stairway is a great accessory for a raised deck. You should be able to buy timber stair supports – pre–cut to the right rise and tread – anywhere you can find decking boards. If you are not attaching the steps to decking, you will need to hold the stair supports firmly with pairs of timber posts top and bottom.

1 SCREW the stair supports securely to the edge of the deck, allowing at least one support every 300mm across the steps **A**.

2 ADD posts for the handrail at each side of the bottom tread, screwing through the stair support while ensuring the post is vertical **B**. If the stair supports are well fixed to the deck, the posts shouldn't need concreting in place.

3 CUT decking boards to length to make the steps and screw first the risers and then the treads firmly in place with galvanized decking screws **C**. Cut a notch in the bottom board's tread to allow for the handrail support.

4 LASTLY, assemble and install the handrail, base rail and balusters as you would the balustrade around decking (see page 82) but cutting the ends of each element at an angle that matches the rise of the steps **D**.

Lighting

THE WAY in which lighting can alter the mood of a garden at night is nothing short of inspirational, and, while installing hard landscaping in your garden is all about making it accessible and usable, a simple application of light extends that usability late into the evening, creating a relaxed and intimate atmosphere.

Practical and picturesque

THERE ARE a number of ways in which light can be used, and these are divided primarily between functional and aesthetic.

▼ **Choosing to highlight certain natural and structural elements can create a whole new look for your garden after dark.**

Functional garden lighting is used to provide the illumination essential for safe movement and navigation, convenience and security. This might include halogen floodlights, which come on automatically when they detect any movement nearby, smaller spotlights to allow you to see what you are doing while cooking at the barbecue or LED (light–emitting diode) units flush–mounted along the lip of a step to prevent falls.

Aesthetic lighting allows you to have rather more fun. You might like to uplight a spectacular tree fern or dramatic classical statue, cast coloured ripples across a garden wall or even allow your guests to watch the shadows of your fish as they flit through the illuminated waters of your pond.

▲ Sleek architectural lines, stylish planting and understated lights can provide a cool, modern feel.

▼ Here a dramatic combination of route and feature lighting has been used to create high visual impact.

Six ways to light your patio

Uplighting

One of the most simple and dramatic effects, uplighting is produced by placing a single spotlight below a favourite plant or feature. It is perfect for illuminating a canopy of leaves or a decorative archway. The reflected light will give a soft glow to the surrounding garden **A**.

Downlighting

Useful for making a feature of a particular plant, ornament or other item, this can also be used as a security measure over a door or archway, or simply to illuminate an area for entertaining **B**.

Cross lighting

This is a variation of uplighting, but this time with two spots shining at a feature from different angles, creating a more subtle focus with softer shadows **C**.

Floodlighting

This uses powerful lamps to throw a wash of light over an area. Though not the most subtle form of lighting, it is useful if you throw large garden parties or need a motion–sensor–controlled security system. Lights should be mounted high up to avoid glare and maximize the amount of light being cast **D**.

Underwater lighting

This requires specialized lighting equipment (available from most garden centres) and can create fascinating effects. Shine your lights upwards from under a fountain – or from behind a waterfall – for a constantly changing display **E**.

Coloured lights

There's no reason why you should stick with white light, and there are many coloured filters and bulbs available. Don't get too carried away, though – the most effective designs use just a few different colours **F**.

▲ Discreet light fittings can often be the most effective option. Recessed spotlights, for example, won't detract from the elegance of sweeping steps.

The regulations

SAFETY STANDARDS for electrical installations have been in existence ever since 1882, but, prior to January 1st, 2005, they were non–statutory. Someone carrying out electrical work did not need specific qualifications other than they should be a 'competent person'. However, on January 1st, 2005, everything changed when the Institution of Electrical Engineers (IEE) Wiring Regulations, the recognized industry standard, were incorporated into the Building Regulations. Henceforth domestic electrical work – both professional and DIY – came under statutory control and would be regulated under Part P (of Schedule 1 to the Building Regulations 2000). The changes were introduced in order to raise the competence of electrical installers and make it harder for 'cowboy' builders to leave electrical installations in an unsafe condition, potentially leading to fires, injuries and even deaths. Before work commences, the local authority Building Control Department must be informed of any electrical work to be undertaken in a kitchen or bathroom or outside the house – as well as any major electrical work done elsewhere. This might include installing a new circuit or changing a consumer unit. Building Control will then, for a fee, inspect the work to make sure that it complies with the regulations.

Top tip

The new regulations gain their teeth when it comes to selling the house. It is anticipated that solicitors acting for a purchaser will want to see the safety certificates. If they are unavailable it may jeopardize the sale.

Electrical work in a garden

Will the work involve changes or additions to final circuits (ring main or lighting circuit)?

No
The local authority do not have to be notified about repair or renewals or changes of appliances.

Yes
Will it be done by a person registered under a Competent Person Scheme (e.g. NICEIC, NAPIT or CORGI)?

Yes
The contractor will issue an installation certificate and inform building control.

No
Notify the local authority building control department.

Will the work be done by an unregistered competent contractor, with appropriate NVQ or City & Guilds, who can provide an installation certificate?

Yes
A building inspector will accept the installation certificate if satisfied that the work is up to standard.

No
Building control may appoint an approved inspector to carry out the safety test (there will be an additional fee).

Building Regulations (Part P) Completion Certificate

▼ **Areas designed for evening entertaining and relaxation, such as a hot tub, should receive special attention.**

Using a registered installer

THE NEW rules allow householders to bypass the local authority, providing they use an installer registered under the 'competent person scheme'. Contractors can become registered by demonstrating that their work meets the standards required in the IEE regulations. A registered contractor will give you a certificate confirming that their work complies with the regulations, and will also notify the local authority.

These changes do not prevent householders undertaking electrical work themselves, but it is essential to demonstrate that the work meets safety standards. The only way to prove this is to carry out a number of electrical tests that would normally require specialist knowledge and equipment. This is usually beyond the reach of the average homeowner.

There is, however, another option. There are many competent electricians that have not registered under the scheme but are quite capable of carrying out all domestic electrical work, including the testing and issuing of certificates. The building inspector may be prepared to accept the work, providing they are satisfied that it meets the requirements of the former IEE Wiring Regulations (BS7671). However, if the building inspector is not

Top tip

In the long run, it may save time and money to have the work done by a registered installer who is used to working within the regulations, rather than doing the work yourself. If you are in any doubt about your ability to carry out the work safely, you should always call in an expert.

convinced, he may bring in an electrical specialist to carry out the tests, and this will incur an additional inspection charge.

What can you do yourself?

Nevertheless, minor work can still be carried out by householders. The regulations only apply to fixed cables and equipment – the 'installation'. For work consisting of changing accessories and components, such as sockets and switches or replacing a section of damaged cable, there is no requirement to inform the local authority. More extensive work done anywhere other than a kitchen, bathroom or outdoors is also excluded.

A competent person would be able to add light points, sockets and fused spurs to existing circuits and can install or upgrade bonding conductors (earth).

Earthing

It is the nature of electricity that it will always try to complete a return circuit back to the supply company's transformer, taking the path of least resistance. If a more suitable alternative is not available, it will use the earth itself. Someone who touches a live electrical wire will receive a severe – possibly lethal – shock if the electricity is able to travel through their body to the ground.

The earthing system is an important safety feature because it provides a low–resistance route for the electricity to take in the event of an electrical fault occurring. It is made up of a

◀ **You can make the most of unusually shaped and textured plants by lighting them individually, their leaves casting exciting shadows.**

network of conductors that link or 'bond' all metal pipes and appliances to the supply company's earth connection point near the meter. In rural areas, the installation may be earthed using a large metal spike driven into the ground. Under fault conditions, the earth network will carry a large current to earth quickly. This electrical surge will cause the fuse to blow (or the Miniature Circuit Breaker, see page 114, to trip), thereby disconnecting the power and overcoming danger.

In order to conform with the latest electrical regulations, a 16mm earth cable should run from the supply company's connection point to a main earthing terminal block and then on to the earthing bar inside the consumer unit where all the earth cores (electricians refer to them as the Circuit Protective Conductors, or CPCs for short) from the installation cables are connected. The main earthing terminal block must be connected to all metal service pipes – typically those supplying water and gas, but also to any other structural metal parts such as oil pipes and air–conditioning units – using 10mm earth cables. Earth cables are identified by their yellow–and–green insulation and are perfectly safe to touch because, under normal conditions, they do not carry any electricity. Because of this, the electrical regulations allow householders to carry out work on the earthing system.

▼ **Combining light and water can create spectacular effects, though you'll need to use special fittings to do this safely.**

Personal safety

INSTALLING GARDEN lighting can be a dangerous business, requiring a good level of knowledge and some common sense. Many people steer clear of electrical work because of its technical nature and the fear that, if they get it wrong, there could be dire consequences. It is right to treat electricity with respect, because slipshod work could cause injury and even fire. Yet, of all the DIY jobs, dealing with electricity is the least difficult. It does not involve the coordination skills required in areas such as carpentry, and most of the domestic work can be accomplished with a few basic tools.

Don't take risks

What is essential when installing garden lighting is a careful, methodical approach coupled with a basic knowledge of electrics and guidance where necessary. Remember that you are combining electricity with damp conditions; if you are in any doubt about your own competence, or if you don't understand any aspect of the installation process, make sure you take the sensible route and call in a professional electrician to help.

If you are confident that you are up to the job, there are still a number of precautions that you should take. Most importantly, do not take any chances. Particularly, do not assume that the power is off without checking first. Always think through the job from start to finish and make sure that you are prepared for all eventualities. Lay out the components in the garden and 'walk through' the steps that you need to take. Install all the new wiring and components and then isolate the circuit (see opposite) by removing the fuse before you make the final connections.

Top tip

If you decide to call in a professional, you can keep costs down by doing much of the legwork yourself. Any cables that need to be buried will be laid much more quickly if you dig the necessary trenches before the electrician arrives. Also it can be cheaper to supply your own materials, particularly if you shop around for a while.

Miniature circuit breakers

Fitted to most modern consumer units, MCBs (Miniature Circuit Breakers) protect your home wiring from an overload or short circuit. They do this simply by 'tripping' when a fault is detected (an event often accompanied by a loud popping noise). Their major advantage over old-style fuses is that they can be easily reset, rather than requiring replacement. MCBs are rated to protect a circuit with a given current and also by the maximum current they can safely interrupt (the current during a short circuit can be many times higher than that which the circuit is designed to carry).

CAUTION: ELECTRIC SHOCK

- It is generally recognized that a current as low as 1/20 amp (50mA) can be lethal. This is slightly less than the amount required to power a 10 watt bulb.

- An electric shock will occur when a person inadvertently becomes part of an electric circuit. The intensity of the shock will depend on circumstances such as humidity and insulation of clothing, as well as the age and fitness of the victim. A shock can range from a sharp tingling sensation to strong pulsations capable of throwing a person off a ladder.

- Do not touch a shock victim before the power has been switched off or you too may become part of the same electric circuit. If this is not possible, stand on a dry object to insulate yourself from the ground and use something non-conductive, such as a broom, to separate the victim from the source of the shock.

- Call an ambulance immediately. If the person is unconscious you should put them in the recovery position.

▼ **Stepping stones over water can be treacherous after dark, but some subtle lighting will solve the problem.**

Fundamental safety aspects

- **Check the power is off**

Before touching an exposed terminal or a bare wire, double-check that the wire is dead by using an electronic mains voltage tester. Test between positive and neutral and, if there is no response, test between positive and earth to confirm lack of power. Confirm that the tester is working by applying it to a live circuit both before and after the test.

- **Wear rubber-soled shoes**

This is an extra precaution to prevent severe shock, because anyone can make a mistake. Similarly, do not work in damp conditions.

- **Only use proper materials and fittings**

Look for a British Standard number. Check that cables and accessories are adequately rated and in good condition.

- **Fit the correct fuse**

Fuses – or fuse wires or MCBs – act as vital safety features of an electrical system. If a fuse of a higher value than that specified is fitted, it may not cut out if danger occurs.

- **Use good workmanship**

Make sure polarity is maintained. The positive (brown) and the negative (blue) must not be swapped over and must be connected to the specified terminals on electrical accessories. Use a socket tester to confirm the polarity. Make sure electrical terminals are screwed tight, conductors are fully insulated, cables are correctly routed and protected and that any work conforms to the regulations.

- **Double-check the work**

Never be complacent. Always make sure that everything has been correctly done before switching back on.

Fuses

Fuses are perhaps the most basic of the electrical safety devices, fitted to most of the electrical equipment you use in and around the home.

Short for 'fusible device', a fuse is a piece of conductive material that will carry a current up to a given rated level. If the current goes above this (for example, when a power surge occurs) the material in the fuse burns out, quickly interrupting the supply.

Fuses must be replaced after such an event, and it is important that the replacement fuse is correctly matched to the one being removed.

Cable

THE CABLES that are commonly installed in domestic premises incorporate two core conductors for positive and negative (referred to as phase and neutral), plus a third conductor for the earth (referred to as the circuit protective conductor or CPC).

Cable sizes

Cables are normally referred to as 'twin and earth' (T&E) and have a size that relates to the cross–sectional area of the positive or negative wires – the 'twin'. The thicker the core, the more current (amps) can be carried by the cable.

Fixed cable

Flexible cable

Fixed and flexible cables

The flat, stiff cables (above) are intended for general house wiring (fixed), whereas the round flexible cables (below) are intended for connecting appliances to the power supply.

CAUTION: CABLE SAFETY

Cable must be chosen to cope with the current the circuit demands. If the capacity is inadequate the cable will overheat, causing premature ageing of the insulation and becoming a source of potential danger.

Cable colour code

On March 31st, 2004, the colours used to identify the core conductors of fixed cables were changed to be the same as those used for flexible cables – the positive red became brown, and the negative black became blue. All new installations after April 1st, 2006 must be in the new 'harmonized' colours (see below). The protective conductor, or 'earth', remains green and yellow. However, in flat cable, the protective conductor is left as a bare copper wire inside the outer PVC sheath.

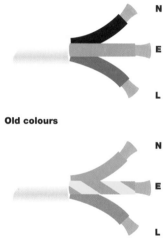

N

E

L

Old colours

N

E

L

New colours

▼ **The age of your electrical equipment will determine the colours of the wiring, but the new system is now more common.**

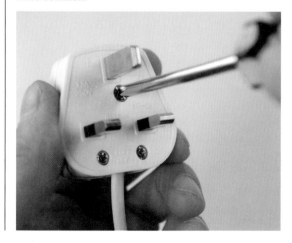

Anatomy of exterior wiring

External lighting circuits are usually very straightforward, with just a few simple rules that you need to follow. You should always protect the circuit with an RCD (see page 120) inside the house, use armoured cable inside rigid plastic conduit and bury the conduit 450mm under the ground – well out off harm's way. If you are unsure about any aspect of the installation, you should ask a qualified electrician to do the work.

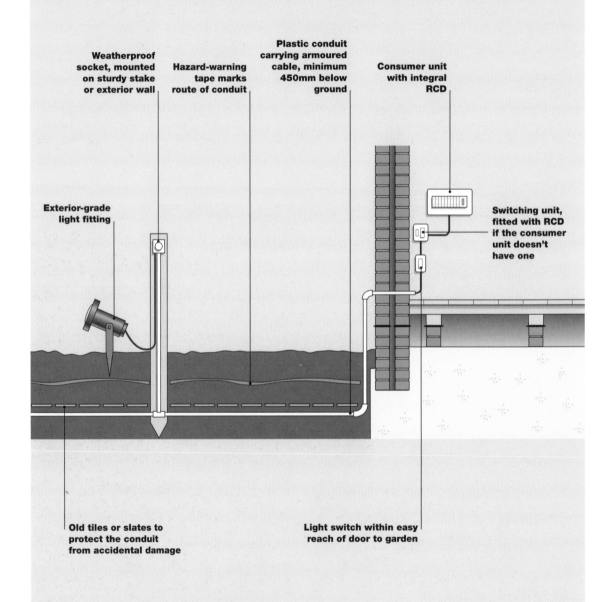

Weatherproof socket, mounted on sturdy stake or exterior wall

Hazard-warning tape marks route of conduit

Plastic conduit carrying armoured cable, minimum 450mm below ground

Consumer unit with integral RCD

Exterior-grade light fitting

Switching unit, fitted with RCD if the consumer unit doesn't have one

Old tiles or slates to protect the conduit from accidental damage

Light switch within easy reach of door to garden

Installing lighting

OUTDOOR ELECTRICS must be connected to the wiring inside your house, but precisely how depends on the lights themselves. Whatever lighting you decide on, however, you must make sure that the lights you buy are recommended for outside use. If you are simply mounting a light on the outside wall of your house, then you can drill through the wall and wire into an existing lighting circuit – or you could use a five–amp fused connection unit (which reduces the current flowing through the wire) to wire into an RCD-protected mains circuit – provided the mains circuit is protected by an RCD at the consumer unit. An RCD (residual current device) will quickly shut down the power supply if it

detects any fault in the wiring. If your fuse box doesn't already have one of these, you should add one specifically for the outdoor power supply.

For lighting further from the house, you should wire into an RCD-protected mains circuit via a five–amp–fused unit connection.

Obviously wiring cannot simply be hidden in the flowerbeds, as it would quickly become snagged and damaged. So you must dig a 450mm deep trench and lay 1.5mm three–core steel–armoured cable, possibly inside special electrical channelling (available from builders' merchants) to allow cabling to be easily replaced in the future. Shield this from careless spades and forks with a layer of protective material (old roof tiles are ideal), and mark the route with hazard–warning tape before refilling the trench.

▼ **Obstacles such as steps are worth lighting generously to ensure they are easy to see.**

Low-voltage systems

Another option is to use a low-voltage lighting circuit, which is probably easier (and certainly safer) to install than a mains set-up. These lights are powered via a transformer that simply plugs into a mains socket inside the house or garage. The transformer must be kept indoors (be aware that they can get quite hot), and the wiring comes out through a hole drilled in the wall.

As the voltage is much reduced there is no danger of getting an electric shock, but, to avoid having loose cables crossing the garden, these should ideally be buried in the same way as the cabling for a mains circuit. Some low-voltage systems even come with a remote-control device, so you can adjust the lighting from the comfort of your patio.

Solar-powered lights

Perhaps the easiest type of lighting installation is a simple photovoltaic unit, which generates energy during the day in order to power a small lamp through the night. One of their most attractive features is that they need no external wiring or site preparation – you simply take the unit out of its packaging and place it in the garden. The amount of light that they produce may not be comparable to a mains system, but the technology involved has come a long way in the past few years, and solar lamps available today are now more than capable of casting enough light to illuminate a pathway or small garden feature.

For the ultimate in ease of use, some designs include a daylight sensor, so that the light comes on automatically as evening draws in. These are often used along the edges of a path, creating a safe, subtle illumination where people will most often need it.

Remember that solar lighting is not necessarily the most eco-friendly option. They don't rely on mains power because they have a built-in battery, which needs to be carefully recycled when the lights no longer work.

Residual current device

An RCD (which stands for Residual Current Device) is a simple safety mechanism that will switch off the power supply to a circuit immediately if it detects a 'leakage' of current. In more simple terms, if the RCD measures a drop in the return current (such as when a short circuit is taking place, potentially via your body) then it switches off the circuit. It does this so quickly that the escaping electricity has no time to do serious damage. An RCD should always be used when working with electricity outside and can be built into the consumer unit (often called the fuse box) or fitted between the appliance and the plug socket.

Switching off the power

NEVER TAKE the risk of working on a circuit that is live. Before cutting any existing wiring or touching any exposed wires, always take the following steps to make sure that you cannot receive an electric shock and use an electronic mains–voltage tester to double–check that you have disconnected the correct circuit.

1 BEFORE starting any electrical work, always switch off the power by turning off the main switch on the consumer unit **A**.

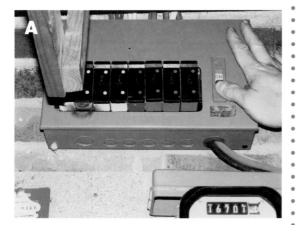

3 ONCE you have removed the relevant fuse, turn the consumer unit's main switch back on again **C**.

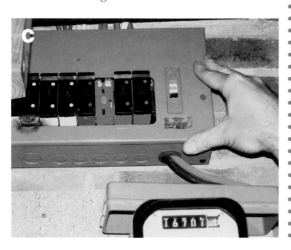

2 LOCATE the fuse for the circuit on which you will be working and remove it **B**.

4 IF MCBs are fitted in place of rewireable fuses, tape the MCB switch in the off position to prevent someone inadvertently turning it back on **D**.

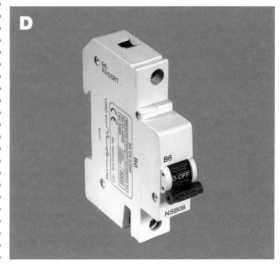

Water features

IN THE past few years, water has become a central element in landscape design, to the extent that you'd be hard–pressed to find a garden makeover show that doesn't include at least a mini pond or a wall fountain.

Manufacturers have been quick to catch on to this phenomenon, and now offer a bewildering array of pond liners and related equipment. Meanwhile, gardeners show no sign of losing their enthusiasm – a fact due in part to the low cost and easy installation of many of these features.

▼ **A pond can be used to neatly define the edges of a patio, and here it separates the clean lines of the paving from an area of planting.**

Tranquil focus

PONDS WORK well with decking and patios, as they are a great source of peaceful entertainment, and the sound of running water can be very relaxing. The constant, gentle burble of a fountain is also an effective means of masking noise such as the neighbours' children or traffic on a nearby road. A raised pond is also a clever way of adding a vertical element to your paving, defining one edge and perhaps even providing a seating area if the walls are wide enough.

Top tip

A pond should be sited in a sunny but sheltered spot away from deciduous trees, because fallen leaves will quickly rot and pollute the water.

▲ Even the simplest water feature can provide hours of quiet entertainment, as wildlife of all shapes and sizes will be drawn to the water.

◄ An ambitious combination of hard landscaping, water features and imaginative planting provides an excellent focal point for any garden.

▼ Running water makes a very soothing sound and is a great way to mask background noise such as traffic.

Construction techniques

THERE ARE two main methods of constructing a garden pond: one uses a rigid liner, the other a flexible one. The rigid variety has a preformed shape, often irregular but sometimes geometrical – such as a circle or square. If used in the ground this type requires an excavation exactly the same shape as the liner, which is then dropped neatly into place. A flexible liner is a sheet of waterproof material such as PVC or butyl rubber. With this option, you can make a pond of any shape or size, allowing you to create a far more natural effect.

In both cases, you should be careful not to puncture or stress the fabric – remove all stones and sharp objects from the excavation and consider installing a protective layer of

sand or specialist landscaping fabric (available on a roll from DIY stores) between liner and soil. While a raised pond might seem like more work, remember that you'll need to do much less digging and disposing of topsoil. The other advantage is that the contents are much closer to eye level, so that you can more easily enjoy fish and plants.

◀ **Though the subtle design of this wall fountain takes up little space, it still provides plenty of visual impact.**

▼ **A flexible liner allows considerable freedom when it comes to designing a pond, stream or waterfall.**

▲ **Simple geometry can be highly effective, as this circular raised brick pond demonstrates.**

Moving water

A LARGE PART of the appeal of a pond lies in the opportunity to create fountains, streams and waterfalls in or around it. Any system of moving water requires a pump, and there are a great many different kinds on the market. A simple fountain pump will sit just below the surface of the water, creating a jet in one of a number of patterns (most come with adjustable or interchangeable nozzles). Streams and waterfalls are a bit more complex, as you need to consider the volume of water you wish to move and the 'head' or height above the pond surface that you wish to reach. A tall, gushing waterfall at the mouth of a long stream will require a more powerful pump than a slower trickle just a little way above the surface. A good aquatics shop will have staff able to help you choose the right system. Remember that you can use one pump to power several features at the same time if it is strong enough, and that it's always a good idea to allow a little extra power in case you need to increase the flow.

Top tip

To keep your water clear, use plenty of hungry plants (ideally so the surface of the water is half covered) and don't buy too many fish.

Always allow slightly more capacity in pumps and filters than you think you will need. The excess will do no harm and could come in useful.

Pond filtration

An UNSTOCKED pond will usually be kept pretty clean by the roots of aquatic plants taking nutrients from the water, but fish are not designed to live in such a restricted environment, and they will excrete far more pollution than your plants can deal with. This can result in murky green water (as algae feed on the excess nutrients), not to mention health problems for your fish.

Filter choices

The answer is to invest in an artificial filter, which will help to keep your water crystal clear. These come in three types (or, more commonly these days, one filter will have three stages). The first is mechanical – essentially it uses sponge, mesh or brushes to sieve the water, removing large particles and long strings of algae. You will probably have to wash out this part of the filter medium regularly, though some designs have clever self-cleaning systems to reduce maintenance. The second stage is biological, which uses bacteria to break down the pollutants in the pond into something less harmful. It is important to keep the water flowing through this stage at all times, otherwise the bacteria will die and the filter will be ineffective until a new colony is established. Lastly, some modern filters include an ultraviolet lamp that kills algal cells by passing the water past a strong UV light. Your filter system will require its own dedicated pump, allowing you to turn off fountains and other features while maintaining a constant flow through the tank.

▼ **Water gardening is great fun, and gazing into a pond can keep you happily occupied for hours.**

Container ponds

IF A full-sized garden pond is beyond your ability or budget, a smaller version can be created in any waterproof container without the complicated electrics needed for a pump and filter. A container pond has many of the advantages of a full-sized pool. It will act as a magnet for wildlife – which is perhaps the easiest way to get children involved in gardening while simultaneously educating them about the richness of our natural environment. All you need to do is line the container with clean pebbles or gravel then add a few well-chosen aquatic plants and fill with water. This is an easy project, requiring no heavy lifting or digging, and is ideal for a small space such as a balcony or by the back door. Not only is it quick to make, attractive and versatile but the materials to create such a simple feature are readily available and won't break the bank.

Top tip

If possible, construct container ponds in their final position, since they can be quite heavy and difficult to manoeuvre once full of water, pebbles and plants.

One for the children

Robust and colourful rubber tub trugs make wonderful child-friendly container ponds, ideal for growing an interesting collection of marginal aquatic plants. Another good option is an old butler sink – you simply need to block the plughole with exterior-grade sealant. Reducing the depth of your container with cobbles or gravel makes it a safer option than a larger body of water, and it should still prove attractive to aquatic insects.

▼ **A pond need not be a grand concern; a simple sink or other water-tight container may provide just what you need.**

Planting your pond

THERE IS a huge range of plants to choose from when you are looking to add some greenery to your pond. On a small scale, however, you'll make most impact if you use strikingly architectural or unusual plants. Some species can be quite invasive, but don't let this put you off; in the confines of a small pond they'll be easy to control – as long as you remember to do it. Native British wildflowers such as ragged robin, marsh marigold or water forget–me–not are good choices, not least for the insect life they will attract.

Varying depth

Many rigid pond liners have built–in planting shelves to make arranging your greenery easier – indeed, a bit of clever digging at the excavating stage will create the same effect for a flexible liner. If you want to raise the level of a plant, you can support it on bricks or an upturned terracotta flowerpot.

▼ **A water garden gives you the opportunity to grow a whole new selection of attractive plants.**

Top tip

Consider using aquatic planting baskets for your plants. These will help keep the water clean and allow you to easily remove or rearrange the plants in your pond.

Plants for ponds

CHOOSING YOUR plants is one of the most exciting parts of creating a pond, but it pays to be armed with a little basic knowledge on the subject. One of the most important characteristics to watch out for is the 'planting depth' of each variety. While pond plants can be divided into rough groups – such as 'floating', 'aquatic', 'marginal' and 'bog' – this does not really supply enough information.

A good supplier should label their stock with more accurate information – some plants just like to have their roots in damp but freely draining soil, others are happier in a given depth of water,

perhaps 5, 10 or 20 centimetres. Even the proper aquatics (water lilies, for example) don't like to be too deep at first but can be moved to deeper water as they grow.

Year-round glory

If you are clever you might also consider seasonal interest. It is easy to have ten plants in flower in the middle of July, but what will the pond look like in winter? Aim to include early- and late-flowering plants to spread your enjoyment, and add a few winter performers – such as a bright-red-barked dogwood (*Cornus alba* 'Sibirica') or a striking white willow (*Salix alba* 'Golden Ness') – near the edges.

Planting medium

You may also need to buy a selection of aquatic planting boxes, baskets and pots. These are simple plastic containers that have lots of holes in each side to allow water in and (in time) roots to grow out. Don't use standard compost when potting-up; it is far too rich and will be bad for

▼ **Making an artificial pond look natural is a bit of a challenge, but, with the right use of plants and materials, it can be done.**

Top tip

Green water is a common problem in garden ponds. It is caused by single-celled algae that multiply rapidly when there is an excess of nutrients in the water. By adding lots of hungry plants you can reduce the free nutrients and eventually clear the water. Surface-shading plants such as water lilies, water hyacinth and water lettuce also help by preventing sunlight from reaching the water – aim to have 30 to 50 per cent of the surface covered.

the pond's natural balance. Opt instead for a specialist aquatic compost, which is relatively low in nutrients. If you can't find this, then plain garden soil will do the trick, provided it's not too rich and hasn't been treated with a weed-killer, fertilizer or other chemicals.

Five top pond plants

Marsh marigold (*Caltha palustris*)

The cheery yellow flowers of this plant are some of the first to appear in spring, a welcome sight when the rest of the garden is still looking wintry **A**.

Water lilies (*Nymphaea*)

These fabulous plants are easy to grow, and to stunning effect. A single pygmy variety can be grown successfully in a large container, and should produce beautiful floating blooms throughout the summer months **B**.

Horsetail (*Equisetum hyemale*)

Using this plant around your pond will prove just as effective as using a multitude of smaller ones **C**.

Purple loosestrife (*Lythrum salicaria*)

One of Britain's most attractive wildflowers, this native plant sends up spires of pretty pink flowers in midsummer **D**.

Pickerel weed *(Pontederia cordata)*

While its name isn't that inspiring, this is an impressive plant for a boggy margin. It grows to 90cm in height and has spikes of blue flowers **E**.

Keeping fish

For some people, keeping fish is the main reason for building a pond. You should bear in mind, however, that you will have far less aquatic life as a result (most fish will gobble up insects and tadpoles before you've noticed they're there). A dedicated wildlife pond is a great idea – you'll get just as much pleasure from watching the natural inhabitants as you would from keeping fish. If you do decide you would like to stock the pond, go for one

Top tip

Don't add any fish until the plants, filtration and water chemistry have reached a natural balance – leave at least two weeks after building the pond.

of the more robust species, such as common goldfish, comets or golden orfe. These tend to have fewer health problems than more exotic breeds and are just as much fun.

▼ **A waterfall provides an excellent way of keeping your pond well-oxygenated, which is especially important for larger fish in hot weather.**

▲ **This beautiful scheme makes use of all types and scales of planting, from the tree-lined backdrop to the marginal and aquatic plants by the pond.**

Fish need room

Much as you might like to, it's not a great idea to keep fish in a container pond. Not only will they be short of space to swim around in but the pollution that they create will overload such a tiny ecological system. Apart from this, the small volume of water and the fact that it lacks the insulation of surrounding soil will cause the temperature in the pond to rise and fall rapidly, which is not great for the health of any fish.

A garden pond

THE PERFECT draw for garden birds and other wildlife, a natural–looking pool is a straightforward DIY project and makes a particularly beautiful and interesting focal point for your garden. You may wish to create an area of deep water or a series of terraces, to allow you to keep plants at different depths in the water.

1 USE timber pegs and a length of hosepipe or line of sand to mark out the shape of your pond on the ground **A**. Stand back and look at the design from a distance to check you are happy with its size and position.

2 EXCAVATE the pond down to the desired depth then excavate further and lay a concrete pad across the base **B**, so that the top of the concrete is level with the intended bottom of the pond.

3 LAY landscaping fabric (or old carpet, if you happen to have some) over the concrete, then carefully spread the liner over the top. Slowly fill the liner with water – checking that the edges don't get pulled down – to hold it in place **C**.

4 LASTLY, hide the edges of the liner with rocks and pebbles (on more landscaping fabric if they have sharp edges) and stock with plants **D**. Note the stepping stones (bottom left of picture) giving easy access to the water.

A raised brick pond

A HIGH–LEVEL POND built next to your patio creates the perfect conversation piece, and the sound of running water is a wonderful accompaniment to a summer evening's entertainment.

1 MARK out the dimensions of the pond using pegs and string or, for curved walls, marker paint, a hosepipe or a line of sand. A flexible liner construction is the easiest option here, as it can be made to fit the shape of your design.

2 DIG down 400mm across the whole area of the proposed pond and line the base of this excavation with 70mm of compacted hardcore. Cover with a thin layer of sharp sand – to fill any gaps – and then 25mm of concrete. Allow it to set hard.

3 LAY an inner wall of 100mm concrete blocks around the edges of the concrete pad **A**. Raise the inner wall to a maximum of 600mm above ground level.

A

4 EXCAVATE and build a second footing, 100mm deep, at ground level around the outside of the concrete blocks. Allow this to set, and then build an outer (or 'facing') wall of your chosen bricks or stone to the same height as the blocks.

5 LAY blocks against one or more interior walls to create plant shelving. Cover all the inner surfaces with a protective layer of landscaping fabric and then add the liner. Fill the pond with water to pull the liner gently into place.

6 CAP the walls with paving slabs on a bed of mortar, trapping the edges of the liner

Top tip

It is important not to raise the inner wall of your pond higher than 600mm above ground. Any higher than this, and the weight of the water could push the walls over.

beneath. If you fix a plastic tube into the mortar beneath the cap, you can run wiring for a pump discreetly into the pond through this.

Furnishing your patio

WITH THE hard work of construction out of the way, the fun of furnishing your deck or patio can begin. A typical 'shopping list' might include a table and six chairs, a decent barbecue, an assortment of beautiful plants and containers and perhaps even the odd statue or piece of sculpture. It's obviously easy to spend money here, but you can shop cheaply too if you use your head. Hold off from buying larger items until the end of the summer, and you may well be able to pick up a bargain simply because the managers of garden centres and DIY stores know sales will soon drop. Also, by buying young plants and 'growing them on', rather than paying for fully grown specimens, you will save yourself some money, not to mention the effort required in taking large plants home in the car.

Taste and scale

THERE IS a size and style of patio furniture to suit every garden, and you should keep both those things in mind when shopping around. With regard to size, measure your patio, and consider carefully how much room you need to leave for movement around obstructions and how easy it will be to get in and out of seating areas. It's no good buying the biggest table you can find if everyone has to get up each time one person wants to get past.

▼ **Size your furniture to the space available and consider a collapsible design in the tightest spots.**

▲ **Furniture takes up more space when in use, so think about how guests will get to and around it.**

▼ **Just one small, elegant seat, for instance, is quite enough at the end of a rustic pathway.**

The style you choose is simply a matter of personal taste, but it's best to try to match that of your patio and wider garden. Timber, rattan and cloth work well with natural–looking gardens, while a more contemporary metal design might suit a chic urban courtyard or deck. Think also about how you will use the furniture. If you intend to do a lot of entertaining, you may need a table that extends for added seating, and, if the patio is not covered, you should consider a sun shade or umbrella. Another important consideration is security – thefts from gardens have reached an all–time high lately, and even bulky items are at risk. If you're spending hundreds or even thousands of pounds on a beautiful set of table and chairs, it's probably wise to spend another five or ten on a lock for the back gate.

Swing seats and hammocks

IS THERE anything more relaxing than the simple luxury of lying in a gently rocking hammock on a quiet Sunday afternoon? While a table and chairs must be the number–one purchase for utility, a more self–indulgent purchase can really make a garden feel like home. Perhaps the main drawback here is the space required – a swing seat will need room for movement in front and behind, while a hammock must be strung from two fairly distant points. If you plan for this when designing your garden, however, you will most definitely find that a compromise on space is well worth it. As these are such seasonal items, you should also consider storage through the winter. Some models

Top tip

If you're planning to attach your hammock to a smooth post or around the trunk of a tree, it is best to use a hook. Otherwise you may quickly find yourself back on the ground.

(particularly those with a tubular metal frame) may be easily dismantled and packed away, while others (such as the heavier timber designs) may be better off under a waterproof cover.

▼ **One of life's most relaxing experiences is lying in a hammock in a beautiful garden.**

Environmental concerns

THERE ARE many things to consider when choosing which furniture you should take home, but the environment is not necessarily an obvious one. In fact, the outdoor furniture market has not always been well regulated and is responsible for stripping some parts of the world (notably Indonesia) of ancient rainforest. While this practice is now more tightly controlled, you should still take responsibility for checking the source of any timber you buy. The FSC (Forest Stewardship Council) mark is a good start, but many people believe we should stop buying some timber, particularly teak, altogether. Look instead for products made from wood harvested in Europe – or consider buying second hand.

▲ This widely recognized symbol indicates that the timber used in the manufacture of a product has been responsibly sourced.

▼ Sometimes the simplest design is just what is called for. If you are buying wooden furniture look for the FSC mark.

▲ **Plants, mellow lighting and elegant furniture combine to create a relaxed and inviting atmosphere.**

Warmth and light

OUR TEMPERATE climate is not always conducive to life outdoors, but there are ways of extending the 'patio living' season. One of the cheapest is simply to shelter the patio from the wind using trellis, planting or even fabric screens. This can make you feel several degrees warmer and will also add a sense of privacy. Another idea is to install a wood–burning clay oven (great for cooking home–made pizza) or a fire pit (which can often double as a barbecue). Apart from the warmth these produce, you will

◀ **Even a small space can be transformed by the right furnishings, creating an intimate 'room outside'.**

also find the patio is bathed in an attractive light. You can extend this lighting style by using candles and oil–burning torches around the perimeter of the seating area, and some citronella–scented varieties of these will also serve to repel mosquitoes.

One purchase you should try to avoid is a gas–powered patio heater. While they certainly warm up the area immediately adjacent to them, they run on a fossil fuel, and the heat is quickly lost to the night sky. Environmental campaigners rank using these gas guzzlers somewhere alongside driving a two–tonne 4x4 to drop the kids off at school!

◀ **Eating 'al fresco' is more popular now than ever. This incredible outdoor kitchen makes entertaining easy, and it looks great too.**

Eating outside

THINK OF a sunny summer's evening in the garden, and you'll probably find yourself thinking about food and drink too. While complaining about the weather is a national pastime, we do tend to make the most of the sun when it comes out – the first warm weekend of the year is usually accompanied by the delicious smells of dinner 'al fresco'.

It is perfectly possible to cook well on a disposable barbecue, or on a compact design that is easily stored away when not in use. If eating outdoors is something you like to do fairly often, though, you may prefer a more substantial installation, perhaps even a brick–built charcoal oven or fire pit. There are even companies that (at a not inconsiderable price) will design and build a bespoke outdoor kitchen, complete with work surfaces, fridges and gas rings.

▼ **On a much smaller scale you could simply consider adding a barbecue to your patio.**

▲ The simplest and most traditional design of good-quality patio furniture is often the most effective.

▼ On the other hand, with such as range of choices available, why not try out a few designs for comfort and practicality?

▶ When siting your furniture, consider access to and from the kitchen – as well as the views across the garden. If placing your seating area on a raised terrace or decking, such as the one shown here, make sure you consider safety and construct balustrades. Here, posts are in place for balustrades to be added.

Dressing a patio

A PATIO IS not complete until you've added plants. These can be grown in pots and other containers or kept in beds and borders to edge and define the paved space. The advantage of container growing is that you are able to move the plants around whenever the occasion dictates (you can even bring tender plants inside for the winter). Container plants do tend to need a bit more maintenance, though, particularly in terms of watering. Very few plants will survive in containers purely on the water that falls as rain. Border planting is a more long–term option and will allow you to create rather more dramatic displays of massed plants. Of course, there's nothing to stop you combining the two.

Horses for courses

WHEN CHOOSING your plants you should, first and foremost, consider the conditions in your garden. This means thinking about the amount of sun the planting area receives through the day, whether it is exposed to strong winds and how cold it gets on a winter's night. Your soil type and local rainfall are also important, though it is possible to artificially 'adjust' these with fertilizers and irrigation. The key to growing plants successfully is to give them what they want, so only buy those that you're sure will be happy in your garden.

▶ Used creatively, the right setting can provide the perfect backdrop for a sumptuous floral display.

◀ These vibrant daisies, *Doronicum excelsum* 'Harpur Crewe', demonstrate the value of matching plants to your garden design.

▼ Be experimental, and remember that even the most unlikely plant partnerships can prove to be extremely effective.

choosing your style

THE NEXT thing you have to consider is your garden's style – there are plants that work well with some looks but might be out of place with others.

Modern/urban

THOUGH IT appears easy, it is actually very hard to have the restraint required to get this look right. Remember that less is definitely more, and look for a small selection of contrasting plants with an architectural feel (see page 150).

▼ **Clean, straight lines and simple materials are the keys to giving your patio this modern look.**

Cottage garden

THIS LOOK is an old favourite among garden designers, and rightly so. The plants involved are often very old native varieties, or at least ones that have been here so long that they feel like natives now. Delphiniums, *Aquilegia* (grannies' bonnets) and daisy–type flowers such as *Rudbeckia* are all good options and, perhaps surprisingly, can also be combined very effectively with both traditional paving materials (perhaps limestone or brick) and more modern options, including polished granite and white–rendered walls.

▲ A traditional cottage garden design should be overflowing with flowering plants and does not need to look too tidy.

Mediterranean

THE WARM, welcoming look of a terracotta-tiled terrace is the perfect backdrop for sun-loving olives, citrus and grapes – any of which might even give you a crop in a good year. For visual appeal you simply can't beat the vibrant flowers of hibiscus and bougainvillea.

Tropical

POPULAR IN recent years, plants such as banana palms, yuccas and tree ferns will all grow in the UK climate if given some protection over the winter. Put them out in spring after the last danger of frost has passed, then cover them with garden fleece or bubble wrap, tied on with string, when winter draws in.

Edible

HERE'S A novel twist. Why not use your patio planting space to grow fresh fruit, vegetables and herbs? You could raise leaf salads in the shade and tomatoes against a sunny wall, then pick both 'live' during a garden party to accompany the food you're cooking on the barbecue. Many types of fruit tree will be happy in large containers as will strawberries and currants. Most suited to the hot, dry conditions of a sunny patio are herbs such as rosemary, oregano and thyme.

◀ Colour and texture are central to an effective Mediterranean design – think about combining warm earth tones and rich terracottas.

Five top architectural plants

Agave

Requiring full sun and well–drained soil, agaves often do well in containers on a hot patio **A**.

Canna lily

The large, exotic leaves and spectacular flowers of the canna are a winning combination. They may need winter protection in colder areas **B**.

Bamboo

There are many types of bamboo to choose from, including some with striking black stems. They are best kept in a pot, as they can be very invasive **C**.

Eucalyptus

An excellent low–maintenance option for contemporary spaces, eucalyptus provides an easy way to give your garden a sense of chic, modern elegance **D**.

Tree fern

Tree ferns are surely the ultimate for a tropical feel. Now widely available, they require some shade and a sheltered position **E**.

Though it is one of the easiest parts of the garden to look after, hard landscaping will still benefit from a little TLC. Prompt action is the key to keeping your workload down. Anything spilt or dropped should be removed before it stains, and weeds should be eradicated before they can take root too firmly. Apart from this, a little light maintenance at regular intervals should keep your paving in top condition.

Cleaning & Maintenance

Looking after your patio

A NEW PATIO or deck will transform your garden and, like most hard landscaping, requires very little maintenance compared with lawn and flowerbeds. That is not to say, however, that it's completely maintenance free, but, by performing a few easy jobs, you can keep it looking at its best. A sensible care routine might involve checking a patio for weeds and giving it a light sweep once a month – then perhaps washing it more thoroughly twice through the summer. Mortared joints

▲ Decking should be treated regularly with a preservative to protect it from the weather and general wear and tear.

should last several years before they require repointing (though you could check them each time you sweep), while joints filled with sand might need topping up every year or two.

Decking should be cleaned at about the same frequency, but it's a good idea to repaint or preserve the timber regularly, perhaps every second year, depending on wear and exposure. You should be particularly careful not to let any algae build up on your decking, as it can become dangerously slippery.

◀ Little and often is usually the easiest and best approach to patio maintenance, keeping the surface free from dirt and leaves.

Cleaning

IF YOUR patio isn't too big, sweeping and washing it shouldn't take longer than an hour or so. It's important to brush away any loose grit first, to avoid scratching the surface. Use warm soapy water and a scrubbing brush or broom, rinsing down well with clean water – or use a pressure washer to blast dirt away.

If you can't face this job (or if your paving covers a large area) you may wish to employ a cleaning company to do the work for you. They will have specialized equipment to give the job a professional finish, and may even be able to re–sand the top surface of your paving, making it look as good as new.

▼ **A pressure washer is a quick way of cleaning many hard surfaces in the garden and can have other applications around the home.**

Pressure washer

While a hose, or even a mop and bucket, will be up to some patio cleaning jobs, you'll get a much more professional result if you use a pressure washer. These have recently become very popular and have therefore dropped in price, but you can still hire one if you're on a tight budget or don't have the space to store one.

They work by pumping water at high speed through a small nozzle, blasting grease, algae and other types of dirt away. When the high-pressure water jet is combined with surface dust and grit, it can badly scratch some materials, so do remember to sweep your patio thoroughly first.

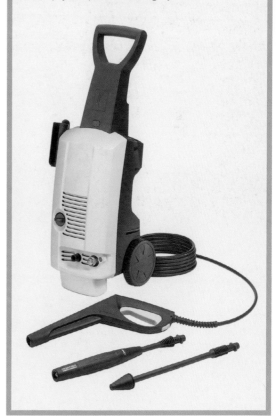

Dealing with stains

As STONE and wood are both porous, they will soak up anything that is spilt on them, something that is likely to happen sooner or later. The important thing to remember is to act quickly before the stain dries out. If all else fails, stains in timber can usually be sanded away, but blemishes on stone will be impossible to remove.

Five common stains

Algal growth

One of the most common causes of patio staining, algae will grow wherever conditions are slightly damp and sunny (i.e. most of the garden!). It is very common around the base of plant pots (which are kept moist), leaving behind green rings when you move the pots. Use a proprietary algaecide as directed on the packaging.

Bird droppings

These are usually washed away quickly by the rain, but, if they are building up in a particular spot, it is because birds are perching somewhere directly above. The build-up can be unsightly on its own, but may also lead to discolouration of a

▲ Food and drink spills are inevitable but should disappear if you tackle them quickly.

stone patio. Scrape or wash them away as soon as you can and remove the overhanging branch or perch to encourage the birds to rest elsewhere.

Efflorescence

A natural process by which mineral salts emerge from the paving, leaving strange white patches (often with the appearance of tide marks). While it is possible to buy cleaning products to remove these marks, it isn't necessary, as they go naturally after a short while.

Food and drink spills

Inevitable on a well-used patio, these are best dealt with as quickly as possible. Scrub the stain with warm soapy water and, if anything remains, wash with one part bleach to ten parts water, then rinse thoroughly.

Oil

Blot the stain quickly with absorbent paper or cloth to remove as much as possible (do not wipe or scrub, or the stain will spread). Cover the stain with a dry powder such as talc and leave it for 24 hours. Repeat until the stain has lifted or, if necessary, use a proprietary cleaner.

◄ If leaves are allowed to build up they will soon rot down and stain your paving. Clear them away quickly before any harm is done.

Weeding

THE JOINTS between paving slabs, setts and bricks should last for years without any maintenance, but, as they get old and worn, they may start to trap wind–blown dirt and dust. This can lead to weeds taking hold, and it is very important to remove these as soon as they start to appear. Weeds left to grow will send down strong roots, opening the joints further and eventually damaging the structure of the path or patio.

Small weed seedlings can usually be pulled up quite easily by hand if you catch them early, but more established ones are often more difficult to remove. Some people find that a patio knife is ideal for digging these out, though you should be careful not to damage the paving itself when you are using it.

You may also find that moss starts to grow on shady areas of the paving. This is much less harmful than other types of weed, and it may even fit with the look of your garden, but, if you want to remove it, you can easily do so with a good stiff broom.

▼ **Weeds can take root between paving elements. Get them out before they do lasting harm.**

Patio knife

The most frequent maintenance job you will need to perform on a brick or slab patio will be weeding. Even if the patio has completely impermeable foundations, it is still likely to collect dust and dirt in the joints, which can then harbour weed seeds. A simple way to clear these out is with a patio knife, which you drag through all the cracks to cut roots and excavate dirt. Make sure you remove all weed growth before it gets too large, as the roots can force apart mortar and concrete in a remarkably short space of time.

Painting and preserving

ECKING IS usually made from pressure-treated timber, which will endure some time without any attention. It will last much longer, however, if you give it a good clean every year or two and coat it with a specialist decking preservative. This will not only keep the timber in good shape but will also greatly improve the look of your deck and help prevent the build-up of unsightly algae.

It is also possible to paint your decking and other wooden structures to freshen up the look of the garden. Outdoor (or all-weather) paints include a preservative just like any other timber treatment but are coloured to either stain the wood (leaving the attractive grain visible) or coat it completely. Exterior paints are available in a great many colours, and there are now environmentally friendly options too. You will find the paintwork will need to be given a top-up coat at least every third year.

▲ Your decking will last much longer if you coat it with a specialist preservative every year or two.

▼ Both decking and stone will benefit from a clean with a rotating brush, which scrubs the surface with pressurized water.

▼ Furniture benefits from a good clean-up, and wooden pieces will need treating every two or three years.

Fixing a loose slab

IF A single slab works loose or is damaged, you should replace it quickly before neighbouring slabs are weakened. This is an easy job but one that requires the right tools.

Plugging chisel

A plugging chisel has a tapered point, which makes it ideal for breaking and cleaning out old mortar. Simply hold the chisel at an angle against the mortar with one hand and strike the end of it with a club hammer.

If you have the tapered side facing down, the chisel will shave off the top surface of the mortar. Turn the tapered face upwards, and the point will be driven in more deeply.

Do this all around a slab or brick before you attempt to remove it.

1 USING a plugging chisel and a club hammer, carefully chip away the old mortar from all four sides of the slab. You should always wear goggles and gloves for this job, as flying stone chippings can be very dangerous.

2 ONCE all the mortar has been removed, work the point of a spade under the edge of the slab and gently lever one side upwards. You can protect the surface of the adjacent slab with a piece of timber.

3 LIFT the slab up and out of the way and use a club hammer and bolster to break up and remove the old mortar underneath. Make sure the sand in the top layer of the sub-base is still firm, then top it up and re-level as required.

4 MIX up fresh mortar and lay it in the gap. Place the slab back in position, tapping it down with a rubber mallet until it is level with the surrounding surfaces. Brush dry mortar into the joints **A**, and wet the area with a fine spray.

Glossary

Arbour

A shelter (though not always fully covered or enclosed) usually made from timber posts and beams. Often used to surround a seating area and often covered with climbing plants.

Ballast

Usually refers to a mixture of sharp sand and gravel intended for use when mixing concrete. Depending on the makeup of the ballast, most general-purpose concrete will require six parts ballast to one part cement.

Baluster

A single vertical element of a balustrade supporting a rail.

Balustrade

A row of vertical balusters that are held in place by a rail top and bottom. What many people refer to as 'railings'.

Blinding

A thin layer of fine material (such as sand) which is brushed over a coarse surface (such as compacted hardcore) to fill any cracks and gaps. This helps to prevent movement and settlement.

Butyl rubber

A synthetic rubber, impermeable to air and water.

Circuit protective conductor

The earth core of a cable used to connect exposed conductive parts to the main earthing terminal.

Coping stones

A top layer applied to a wall for ornamental purposes and to shed water during rainfall.

Damp-proof membrane

A sheet or strip of impermeable material (often plastic) used to prevent water from penetrating walls, floors or other surfaces.

Fall

A slope or drop across a horizontal surface, often referred to as a ratio. For example, a fall of 1:60 is a 1cm vertical drop in every 60cm.

Footing

The excavations required to build a foundation. Essentially, a hole in the ground, until the sub-base is built.

Hardcore

A mixture of crushed concrete, brick and other hard debris, often recycled from demolition sites. Used to create a cheap but very solid base for most foundations. Must be compacted thoroughly to avoid settlement.

Hard landscaping

Any artificial area of stone, timber or similar material in a garden or other outdoor environment. Concrete patios, decks, brick paths and walls are all good examples.

Joists

The horizontal elements of a frame, such as those used to support decking boards.

Landscaping fabric

A sheet material which is used variously to reduce the growth of weeds, separate and protect other materials (such as pond liners) and help keep loose aggregates in place. Available in various sizes and grades.

Obelisk

A vertical structure used (in a garden setting) either for architectural decoration or as a support for climbing plants.

Perpendicular

At an angle of 90 degrees to a given line, plane or surface.

Photovoltaic unit

A device that can create electricity from sunlight. Often known as a solar panel.

Pilot holes

Small holes drilled into a material to act as a guide for a larger drill bit or for screwed fixings. Also help to prevent timber from splitting when screwed together.

Plant machinery

Larger items of machinery used in construction jobs, such as diggers, plate compactors and motorized wheelbarrows. These are generally best hired, as they are rather expensive to buy.

Pointing

A finishing process involving pushing mortar into the gaps between bricks. This helps to exclude wind and rain and neatens the final appearance of the brickwork.

PVC

Polyvinyl chloride, a common type of plastic used in many applications.

Rail

A horizontal bar, such as those used at the top and bottom of a balustrade.

RCD

Residual Current Device – a safety feature of outdoor wiring circuits.

Riser

The vertical face of a single step, topped with a tread.

Screed

A flat concrete surface. Also a long, straight piece of timber used to flatten concrete.

Sharp sand

Occasionally called grit sand or coarse sand, this is a cheap and easily sourced material used for a wide range of building jobs including mixing concrete and bedding-in paving. It has a high proportion of relatively large particles and a low clay content.

Shim

A small piece of timber used to prop something up. In the case of hard landscaping, this is often precisely measured to help calculate and maintain a desired fall.

Soft sand

Also known as builder's or building sand, this is finer than sharp sand and has a higher clay content. It is used when mixing mortars.

Spacer

Any evenly sized object used to maintain a regular gap between decking boards or paving slabs during construction. Nails or screws are often used for timber, while short lengths of dowel or batten are more practical for stone.

Specimen plants

Individual (or small groups of) plants used as striking highlights, often along a walkway or at the end of a long vista.

Sub-base

The materials which, when placed in a footing, make up a foundation – usually in layers of hardcore, concrete and/or sharp sand.

Subframe

The main structural elements of any frame, including that which is required to support timber decking boards. Consists of a number of vertical posts and horizontal joists.

Travertine

Somewhere between limestone and marble (both visually and geologically), this beautiful stone is at the very top end of the paving–material price range.

Tread

The horizontal face of a single step. It is supported at its leading edge by a riser.

Suppliers

PATIO SUPPLIERS AND INSTALLERS

Bradstone
Bardon Hall
Copt Oak Road
Markfield
Leicestershire, LE67 9PG
+44 (0)1335 372 289
www.aggregate.com

Chris Williams Landscapes
97 Sandy Road
Sandyford
Stoke-on-Trent
Staffs, ST6 5LN
+44 (0)1782 832 324
www.cwlandscapes.co.uk

Stoneflair
Bardon Hall
Copt Oak Road
Markfield
Leicestershire, LE67 9PG
+44 (0)1335 372 289
www.aggregate.com

GARDEN LIGHTING

Lighting for Gardens
7 Dunhams Court
Letchworth Garden City
Hertfordshire, SG6 1WB
+44 (0)1462 486 777
www.lightingforgardens.com

Moonlight Design
Moonlight Design Ltd
Units B and C
Rear of 112 Station Road
London, E4 6AB
+44 (0)20 8925 8639
www.moonlightdesign.co.uk

DECKING SUPPLIERS AND INSTALLERS

Arbordeck
Lincoln Castle
Lincoln Castle Way
New Holland
Barrow-upon-Humber
North Lincolnshire, DN19 7RR
+44 (0)1469 535 427
www.arbordeck.co.uk

Deckbuilders
The Firs,
Hill
Pershore
Worcestershire, WR10 2JZ
+44 (0)845 370 7790
www.deckbuildersltd.co.uk

WATER GARDENING

Oase
3 Telford Gate
Whittle Road
West Portway Ind. Est.
Andover
Hampshire, SP10 3SF
+44 (0)1264 333 225
www.oase-livingwater.com

Tetra
P.O. Box 271
Southampton
Hampshire
SO18 3ZX
www.tetra-fish.co.uk

TOOLS AND MATERIALS

Screwfix
+44 (0)500 41 41 41
www.screwfix.com

CLEANING AND MAINTENANCE

Kärcher
Kärcher House,
Beaumont Road
Banbury
Oxfordshire, OX16 1TB
+44 (0)1295 752 200
www.karcher.co.uk

Spinaclean
Whitworth Chambers
George Row
Northampton
Northamptonshire, NN1 1DF
+44 (0)1604 759 201
www.spinaclean.com

About the author

Paul Wagland is an RHS-qualified gardener and an experienced writer and designer. He specializes in the practical side of horticulture, from landscaping and outdoor DIY to growing fruit and vegetables. With a firm belief that a well-maintained garden can add considerable value to a home, Paul has redesigned and renovated many neglected plots for both enjoyment and profit. Author of *Practical Allotments* and co-author of *The Energy-efficient Home*, both by GMC Publications, he is also the former editor of two popular gardening magazines (*Pond & Gardening* and *Grow Your Own*).

Acknowledgements

All photography by Paul Wagland, with the following exceptions:

T = top, M = middle, B = bottom
L = left, R = right
F = first, S = second, TH = third

Ben Vanheems: 127.

Bradstone: 41.

FSC: 139T.

GMC Publications: 76.

iStockphoto.com: Hagit Berkovich: 150BL; Hilary Brodey: 130BL; CapturedNuance: 141, 142–143; Dan Chippendale: 56; cjmckendry: 106, 129; Andy Dean: 150TL; Yvan Dube: 10TR; Paul Erickson: 109BR; Eira Fogelberg: 71B; fotolinchen: 130BR; Hedda Gjerpen: 130TR; joannawnuk: 138; Jim Jurica: 130TL; Michael Koehl: 14; Susan McBaine: 85; Steven Miric: 101; Missing35mm: 21; modesigns58: 45; Nancy Nehring: 131; Peepo: 117BR; Kathleen C. Petersen: 143R; Ben Phillips: 150BR; Aimin Tang: 150TR; Ann Taylor–Hughes: 145; Taysh: 151; YinYang: 137T.

Japan National Tourist Organization: 126.

Japan Ryokan Association, The garden of Sansuiro Ryokan: 54.

Marston & Langinger: 2; 10TL; 17B; 33TR; 38TL.

Screwfix: 33TL, ML, M, BR, BL; 34; 35; 36; 81B; 114; 116; 120; 157T; 159L.

All illustrations by John Woodcock, with the following exception:

GMC Publications: 117.

Index

To place an order, or to request a catalogue, contact:
GMC Publications
Castle Place, 166 High Street, Lewes, East Sussex, BN7 1XU
United Kingdom
Tel: +44 (0)1273 488005 Fax: +44 (0)1273 402866
Website: www.gmcbooks.com
Orders by credit card are accepted

31901050963109